This signed edition of

THE SEAT OF
THE SOUL

by

Gary Zukav

GARY ZUKAV

has been specially bound by the publisher.

GARY ZUKAV

the

SEAT

of the

SOUL

25th Anniversary Edition

SIMON & SCHUSTER

New York   London   Toronto   Sydney   New Delhi

Simon & Schuster
1230 Avenue of the Americas
New York, NY 10020

Copyright © 1989 by Gary Zukav
Foreword copyright © 2014 by Gary Zukav
Preface copyright © 2014 by Harpo, Inc.
Preface copyright © 2014 by Maya Angelou

This Simon & Schuster hardcover edition November 2017

SIMON & SCHUSTER and colophon are
registered trademarks of Simon & Schuster, Inc.

For information about special discounts for bulk purchases,
please contact Simon & Schuster Special Sales at
1-866-506-1949 or business@simonandschuster.com.

The Simon & Schuster Speakers Bureau can bring authors to your live event. For
more information or to book an event contact the Simon & Schuster Speakers
Bureau at 1-866-248-3049 or visit our website at www.simonspeakers.com.

Interior design by Joy O'Meara
Jacket design by Kathleen DiGrado
Front jacket photograph by Harald Sound/Photographer's Choice/Getty Images
Author photograph by Christopher Briscoe
Interior image from Shutterstock

Manufactured in the United States of America

1   3   5   7   9   10   8   6   4   2

Library of Congress Cataloging-in-Publication Data

Zukav, Gary.
The seat of the soul : 25th anniversary edition /
Gary Zukav.—Simon & Schuster hardcover edition.
      pages   cm
      Includes index.
1. New Age movement.   2. Spiritual life—New Age movement.   I. Title.
      BP605.N48Z85   2014
299'.93—dc23   2014000150

ISBN 978-1-5011-8497-0

This book is dedicated to my parents,
Morris L. Zukav and Lorene Zukav,
with love, respect, and gratitude.

I am grateful for the joyful love, continual support, and endless creativity of Linda Francis, my spiritual partner since 1993 and probably long before. I am amazed frequently—through our tendernesses and power struggles—that I not only love her, but I love loving her. This expanded, reenergized, and rededicated Edition carries within it the commitment that we share to creating authentic power and spiritual partnerships and to supporting people around the world to create them. Thank you, Beloved.

Contents

CONTENTS

Preface to *The Seat of the Soul* 25th Anniversary Edition

by

Oprah Winfrey

I first read *The Seat of the Soul* in 1989.

As with all books I'm excited about, I had also bought copies for my friends and colleagues so everybody could be reading it at the same time. I happened to be the first to finish, which meant I had no one to discuss the book with. So, I got my hands on the Mount Shasta, California, phone directory and called Gary Zukav.

"Mr. Zukav, hello, my name is Oprah. I just want to talk to you about your book and would love for you to come on my show and share your—"

"What did you say your name was?"

"Oprah."

"Could you spell that, please," he said.

I did. "O-p-r-a-h, and the 'h' is silent," I explained. And then I told him that I had a talk show, and had to explain what a talk show was, because Gary had been without a TV for several years. This, of course, made me even more eager to speak with him. I wanted to know how he knew what he knew. The things he'd written resonated so deeply with me, and felt so true, but how did he know for sure?

——— ———

The Seat of the Soul changed the way I see myself. It changed the way I view the world. It caused a profound shift in the way I conduct all my relationships, business and personal.

The book came to me at the perfect time—at a moment in my life when I was ready for and open to more. More connection. More harmony. More peace. More joy. I could sense that there was more to our existence than day-to-day experiences and the rituals of work and relationships, more to life than our five senses could hold.

The Seat of the Soul put into words what my own soul already knew and had been trying to tell me. It was such an exhilarating awakening to see affirmed in print what I hadn't discovered the language to articulate myself. When I first read the words "multisensory perception," I felt as though Gary had touched a nerve. In fact, the book felt like one great multisensory explosion. Everywhere I looked after reading it, I saw and experienced life in a new light.

Gary's book was one aha moment after another, all steering me in the direction of true north. My favorite insight: "When the personality comes fully to serve the energy of its soul, that is authentic empowerment."

It's no big secret that I have a big personality. I've been using it to my advantage since the third grade. But using that personality to serve my soul—and making sure the two were aligned—changed the way I did everything. I suddenly recognized all the times I'd gotten off track by letting my personality rule. I started to notice that the degree to which I ever felt unhappiness, discomfort, or despair was in direct proportion to how far I let myself stray from the seat of my soul.

The chapter that stirred me most was the one about intention. These words became my living creed: "Every action, thought, and feeling is motivated by an intention, and that intention is a cause that exists as one with an effect. If we participate in the cause, it is not possible for us not to participate in the effect. In this most profound way we are held responsible for our every action, thought, and feeling, which is to say, for our every intention." Those words changed my life.

Prior to reading *The Seat of the Soul,* I suffered from the disease to please. Like millions of people, most of them women, I was a slave to the needs, wants, and desires of others. I would say yes when I seriously wanted to say no. I would give precious time and energy, money, gifts—whatever was asked—simply to avoid the possibility of upsetting someone. I once flew from Chicago to Spain, appeared onstage for less than forty-five seconds at a friend's charity benefit, then got back on a plane and flew straight to work to do my show—all because I didn't know how to say no. To this day, I couldn't even tell you what the charity event was for.

This sort of thing used to happen to me a lot. My life was a whirlwind of one event after another, nonstop speaking engagements, appearances for almost anyone who asked. I wanted people to like me. And as long as I gave them what they wanted, I suppose they did.

My breakthrough was recognizing that my intention to be liked was causing all the requests. Cause and effect. If your intention is to do what other people want, they will keep asking you to do exactly that. That was an aha moment! When I changed my intention to be about doing what I wanted, what I felt was worthy of my time, the effect automatically changed.

Twenty-five years later, today, for me, moving with intentional purpose is like breathing, but I had to learn the practice from the pages of *The Seat of the Soul*. Gary Zukav's principle of intention fundamentally altered my every action. It even changed the consciousness of *The Oprah Winfrey Show*. When we first started, producers would present their ideas in a weekly pitch session, but after encountering Gary's ideas from *The Seat of the Soul*, I created a new policy. For all the producers, I would say: State your intention for the show first. Why do you want to do it? What do you want the outcome to be?

Sometimes producers—who had to fill two hundred

show slots a year—would make up an intention just to appease me, and I would say, "Nope, not a good enough reason." Even if the intention had no redeeming value other than, "We just want to entertain people and get a high rating," I encouraged all of us to be clear about it. State your case with intention and purpose, and the result will follow suit.

On Gary Zukav's first appearance on my show, in 1998, we discussed the nature of the soul. That interview set my career on a new course. Bringing spirituality to daytime television was uncharted territory. Having a conversation about consciousness, responsibility, intention, and the Law of Cause and Effect was not exactly ratings-busting TV, but I told myself, If not now, when? To be honest, had I not owned and controlled the show, Gary's thirty-six appearances over the years would never have happened. My producers were convinced in the beginning that television wasn't ready for a conversation about the soul.

But the course I took has served me well. And I continue to explore the spiritual side of life on my OWN cable network. Quite frankly, I don't believe I would ever have dreamed of creating such a network had I not read *The Seat of the Soul.*

I've taught leadership classes at the Oprah Winfrey Leadership Academy for Girls with the help of *The Seat of the Soul.* I've used its principles to teach elementary school students, high school students, even MBAs at the Kellogg School of Management. I get a surge of delight every single time someone reads this book and feels the amazement I felt twenty-five years ago. If you're ready to see the world in a new way, if you're ready for your life to open up and change, if you're ready for an exhilarating awakening, I think you'll feel it, too.

Preface to *The Seat of the Soul* 25th Anniversary Edition

by

Dr. Maya Angelou

Courage is the most important of all the virtues because without courage one cannot practice any virtue consistently. We can be kind, generous, just, courteous, and merciful sporadically, but to display those virtues, consistently, calls for an enormous display of courage. From childhood on we have been taught that the heart, the mind, and the personality, the spirit and the soul have come to life together occupying the same space and then they will go together into death.

The intrepid, daring Gary Zukav, in his book *The Seat of the Soul*, introduces a brand-new concept to my mind, or rather a concept which I found in my youthful years in the Negro Spirituals which confused me because the lyrics suggested that pain and joy, weeping and laughing were all together when death came and that they left together to go into death.

The song, however, which often calls God the Soul, informs the listener that the Soul never dies but will continue and bring into life another mind and personality as well as other troubles and joys. They would bear the experience of living until death would relieve them of their responsibility. Then as they died, Soul or God would continue as it could not die.

Zukav, a respectful thinker, is able in his book *The Seat of the Soul* to show the reader how human evolution is achieved by the continuity of the Soul and the ability of a personality to die and another to be born a little better, a little stronger, and a little more daring.

I don't know if the poet in Zukav took his hand and bid him tell the hard truths as easily as willow trees bow gracefully along a brook side. There are some readers who choose books for summer reading and others for vacation entertainment. The reader who chooses *The Seat of the Soul* should put the book on a shelf, near the bed, or on a lamp table which boasts a good strong bulb.

I keep my second copy of the book covered in plastic at the kitchen table, so it will be protected from years of use and so that the olive oil from a just-made salad will not smudge the cover.

After reading Zukav's book for the tenth time, I still found it outrageous. I remembered a play I wrote, called *And Still I Rise*. The two characters in the play (male and female) have died and found themselves in what they think is a waiting room. A ghoulish creature appears. The male character, named Zebediah, says, "I know who you are. You are the gatekeeper. You will take us to the place we are supposed to go—heaven or hell."

The female character, Annabel, adds, "I didn't make it, but I truly tried to live a good life, clean, kind, fair."

The eerie creature starts a little laugh which turns into huge laughter. He gazes at the two piteous-looking characters and says, "I am always amazed, even startled at the condition of human imagination. You think there is only a heaven or hell. Zebediah and Annabel, in your futures alone, there are possibly eight hundred destinations."

In my play, Annabel and Zebediah, who had been sitting separately, move to each other without seeming to notice. Suddenly they are close enough to embrace. And they do.

The lyrics of the nineteenth-century Negro Spiritual are

Soon, I will be done with the troubles of the world,
The troubles of the world,
The troubles of the world,
I'm going home to meet my God.
No more weeping and wailing,
No more laughing and dancing,
No more moaning and crying,
I'm going home to meet my God.

Obviously the poet decided a minutiae of daily life occupies one space and that the true Soul of the poet lives in another space which the poet calls God.

I suggest to the new Zukav reader to draw close to share this book with someone who has firm nerve and a wonderful sense of humor, because when Zukav's ideas stop challenging you, you will laugh with the wonderful laughter of the discoverer who has found a new continent.

No more weeping and wailing.
No more weeping and wailing.
I'm going home to meet my Soul.

Foreword to *The Seat of the Soul* 25th Anniversary Edition

This 25th Anniversary Edition of *The Seat of the Soul* fills me with gratitude and joy. After I finished the manuscript twenty-five years ago, I sat with it wondering whether anyone would read it, and if anyone read it, whether anyone would understand it. In the midst of these thoughts, another thought appeared, louder and clearer. It said, "Do not be concerned. This arrow will find its mark." *The Seat of the Soul* has now found its way to millions of hearts, and the arrow is still in flight.

While writing my first book, *The Dancing Wu Li Masters: An Overview of the New Physics,* I discovered—to my complete surprise—inspiration that came from beyond my mind, nonphysical intelligences that I could not articulate, and the electricity of creating consciously with constructive intent. I had never experienced anything like this. I loved these experiences, but, for the most part, I forgot about them after the book was finished.

FOREWORD TO THE 25TH ANNIVERSARY EDITION

The Dancing Wu Li Masters—which won the American Book Award for Science—established me as a popularizer of modern science. Many people expected me to follow it with a sequel, a *Son-of-Wu-Li-Masters*, that would explain more cutting-edge science. Instead, my next book was about evolution, reincarnation, karma, and the soul. It was about emotional awareness, responsible choice, and intuition. It was about an unprecedented transformation of human consciousness and the emergence of a new power—authentic power. In short, the new book was about a new human species, its new capabilities, and its new potential.

This book was *The Seat of the Soul*. It surprised me more than anyone. Everything remarkable that touched me briefly while I was writing *The Dancing Wu Li Masters* returned undeniably, unmistakably, irrevocably into my awareness. I discovered nonphysical reality. I am still growing into that discovery. All creative people—which is everyone—require commitment and time and courage to grow into their insights. Inspiration is one thing. Applying it to your life is another. My friend Maya Angelou tells me that when people tell her, "I am a Christian," she replies, "Really? Already? I am in my eighties, and I am still trying." Like Maya, I am still learning, still striving to apply the most meaningful insights of my life, and still changing for the better.

Reading *The Seat of the Soul* twenty-five years after it was written was a completely surprising and deeply fulfilling experience. The book seemed perfect. Every sentence carried meaning for me. Soon, almost the entire book was under-lined. I was thirsty for the words. They sank into me like water into dry sand. They nurtured and soothed me. The blessing that I felt when I was writing this book returned to me amplified many times. I basked in it. I thought I knew it all. After all, I typed it, edited it, and talked about it for years. But rereading the book showed me that I had things to remember, more to learn, and much more to practice.

The Seat of the Soul brought remarkable people into my life. Two of them in particular touched me more deeply than I could have imagined and continue to support me in ways that thrill and surprise me.

The first is Linda Francis. I do not remember the first time we met, although she does. We met again a year later at a small retreat where I was speaking. I remember everything about that meeting. I was surrounded by loving people, and I found myself pushing one of them away—Linda. I wanted none of the hugs she gave so freely. This was my first clue that parts of me were threatened by her, but I was not aware enough to recognize it. I could not escape her at the event—for example, a friend saved a seat for me at a concert, a dif-ferent friend saved a seat for Linda, and the saved seats were together. I began to share my curiosity with her. Why was I pushing only her away? I shared my intention not to be controlled by this unusual repulsion. "I will not refuse your love," I told her—not romantic love, but the love that she so obviously felt with her friends at the retreat and that she held out to me as well. At the end of the event, friends invited me to join them for a cold splash in a waterfall. When they suggested that I invite Linda, I became irritated.

Linda! Linda! What is this thing with Linda? Can I not do anything at this event without Linda? When Linda called me a month later to tell me that she was moving to Mount Shasta, California, where I lived—a decision that predated the retreat—I felt frightened and, again, curious. When our friends and I welcomed her to her new home, I was surprised to realize how much I had been looking forward to her arrival! I was relaxed, comfortable, happy, and open. We began to visit each other. Some of our talks I enjoyed, and others I did not, but I found myself looking forward to each one. Several months later the thought occurred to me, "I think I am in a relationship!" Without the sexual interactions that had begun my previous "relationships," new and different kinds of interactions began to occur. These were my first experiences of a substantive and deep relationship for the purpose of spiritual growth—a spiritual partnership. A half year later, about twenty years ago, she moved into my cabin, and our journey together continues today.

In our years together, I have marveled not only that I love Linda—something I did not think myself capable of when we met—but that I *love loving her*! This is the experience that intrigues me. It is as strong in me now as it was when I discovered it. Where does *that* come from?

The second person is Oprah Winfrey. She is the instrument that the Universe chose to explode me out of the backcountry and into the larger world. I suspect that nothing less than that explosion could have done it. She took me into her heart, her creativity, and her famous *The Oprah Winfrey Show*. First, I was a recluse on a mountain, and then, a few months later, I was speaking to ten million people monthly. New friends appeared wherever I went in the world, thanking me for a show, smiling at me from a distance. It took me a long time to acknowledge that my life of isolation was over and even longer to welcome it.

During each show Oprah and I sat before an eager audience and the company of fellow souls around the world. She introduced a theme, asked me some questions, and then, with a gesture of her hand or movement of her face, turned the attention of millions of people toward me. It was terrifying and awesome. "Sacred" and "holy" are better words. When a national magazine pursued me for an article, she counseled, "It's only cotton candy, Gary. Only cotton candy." What could have described external power better? My adopted Sioux Uncle, Phil Lane, Sr., once told me after watching one of our shows, "Nephew, you are talking like the old people." That memory fills me with strength and gratitude. I am grateful for Oprah and to the Universe for all of these experiences and more.

In the years following my shows with Oprah, Linda and I cofounded the Seat of the Soul Institute, gave many events, wrote books, and developed long-term, in-depth programs for small groups. Now our passion for supporting people and spiritual partnerships has grown stronger than ever, but traveling has become taxing for us, so we have created new digital tools and innnovative ways to use the Internet, such as an ongoing support program, eCourse, eNewsletters, an online Spiritual Partnership Community, live videos, and the Web addresses at the end of the Chapter Study Guides in this book. (Tap them in your eBook or type them into your browser and they will take you to Web pages that will help you further explore, integrate, and apply what you are studying.) You will find all of these and more at SeatoftheSoul .com. Linda and I still enjoy giving live events when possible, including our favorite, the annual *The Journey to the Soul* summer retreat. I hope that I will meet you personally at one of them.

The Internet is a reflection in the domain of the five senses of our emerging awareness of our connectedness. It does not create, or even increase, our connectedness. It is not possible for us to be more or less connected than we are with one another and Life. Can a flower be more or less connected to its color? Let us enjoy this beautiful reflection together and also what it reflects.

The most difficult, gratifying, and thrilling experiences I have had since publishing *The Seat of the Soul* have been my experiences of authentic power and creating authentic power. Spiritual partnerships, richness of cocreation, and awe of Life have slowly replaced my experiences of people as things and my tormenting journeys through anger, jealousy, despair, and unworthiness. I still encounter parts of my personality that are angry, frightened, jealous, superior, and inferior, but now I see them as opportunities to create authentic power, to choose anew. If I can do this, you can, too. I know that eventually you will. The transformation of consciousness that is expanding our perception beyond the five senses, redefining power, and showing us the potential of a Universal Humanity is proceeding in full force.

Each choice of fear—anger, jealousy, vengefulness—is a choice to evolve unconsciously through the painful, destructive consequences that fear creates. Each choice of love—gratitude, patience, appreciation—is a choice to evolve consciously through the healthy, constructive consequences that love creates.

Why not choose the conscious path, the path of joy? Why not journey consciously to the seat of your soul—that place where you transform energy into matter with your intentions—infuse your world with love and live there?

All roads lead to home.

Gary Zukav

Foreword to the First Edition

During the years that I was writing *The Dancing Wu Li Masters* and after, I was drawn again and again to the writings of William James, Carl Jung, Benjamin Lee Whorf, Niels Bohr, and Albert Einstein. I returned to them repeatedly. I found in them something special, although it was not until later that I was able to understand that specialness: These fellow humans reached for something greater than they were able to express directly through their work. They saw more than they could express in the language of psychology or linguistics or physics, and they sought to share what they saw. It is what they sought to share through the medium of their work that drew me to them.

They were mystics. That is my word. They would not use such language, but they knew it. They feared that their careers might become contaminated by association with those who did not work within the scientific model, but in the depths of their own thoughts they each saw much too much to be limited by the five senses, and they were not.

Their works contribute not only to the evolution of psychology, linguistics, and physics but also to the evolution of those who read them. They have the capability to change those who touch them in ways that also cannot be expressed directly in the terms of psychology, or linguistics, or physics.

As I came to understand, in retrospect, the magnetic quality that these works held for me, I came to understand that what motivated these men was not Earthly prizes or the respect of colleagues, but that they put their souls and minds on something and reached the extraordinary place where the mind could no longer produce data of the type that they wanted, and they were in the territory of inspiration, where their intuitions accelerated and they knew that there was something more than the realm of time and space and matter, something more than physical life. They knew it. They could not necessarily articulate this clearly, because they were not equipped to talk about such things, but they felt it and their writings reflected it.

In other words, I came to understand that what motivated these men, and many others, was in fact something of great vision that comes from beyond the personality. Each of us is now being drawn, in one way or another, to that same great vision. It is more than a vision. It is an emerging force. It is the next step in our evolutionary journey. Humanity, the human species, is longing now to touch that force, to shed that which interferes with clear contact. Much of the difficulty in doing this lies in the fact that the vocabulary with which to address this new force, which is indeed the eternal force, is not yet born.

In this moment and in this hour of human evolution, this proper vocabulary and means of addressing that which longs to transcend religiosity and spirituality and assume the position of authentic power is longing to be born. We need to give that which we as a species are now touching consciously for the first time a vocabulary that is not clouded, so that it can be identified clearly in the acts and judgments of the human race, so that it can be seen clearly, and not through veils of mystery or mysticism, but simply as the authentic power that moves the force fields of this Earth of ours.

As a way of talking about what we are and what we are becoming, I have used the terms "five-sensory" and "multisensory." Multisensory is not better than five-sensory. It is simply more appropriate now. As one system of human experience winds down and another, more advanced system emerges, the older system may appear by comparison to be lacking, but from the perspective of the Universe, the language of comparison is not the language of lesser and better, but of limitation and opportunity.

The experiences of the multisensory human are less limited than the experiences of the five-sensory human. They provide more opportunities for growth and development and more opportunities to avoid unnecessary difficulties. I have contrasted the experiences of the five-sensory human with the experiences of the multisensory human in each instance to make their differences as clear as possible, but this does not mean that the five-sensory phase of our evolution, the phase from which we are emerging, is negative in comparison to the phase of our evolution that we are entering, the multisensory phase. It is simply that it is now no longer appropriate, just as there came a time when the use of candles became inappropriate because of electricity, but the advent of electricity did not make candle power negative.

Who among us is an expert on the human experience? We have only the gift of sharing perceptions that hopefully can help those on their journey. There is no such thing as an expert on the human experience. The human experience is an experience in movement and thought and form and, in some cases, an experiment in movement and thought and form. The most that we can do is comment on the movement, the thought, and the form, but those comments are of great value if they can help people to learn to move gracefully, to think clearly, to form—like artists—the matter of their lives.

We are in a time of deep change. We will move through this change more easily if we are able to see the road upon which we are traveling, our destination, and what it is that is in motion. I offer what is in this book as a window through which I have come to see life. I offer this window to you, but I do not say that it is necessary that you accept it. There are so many ways to wisdom and to the heart. This is our greatest richness, and the one that gives me the most joy.

We have much to do together.

Let us do it in wisdom and love and joy.

Let us make this the human experience.

Gary Zukav

INTRODUCTION

— 1 —

Evolution

The evolution that we learned about in school is the evolution of physical form. We learned, for example, that the single-celled creatures of the oceans are the predecessors of all more complex forms of life. A fish is more complex, and, therefore, more evolved than a sponge; a horse is more complex, and, therefore, more evolved than a snake; a monkey is more complex, and, therefore, more evolved than a horse, and so on, up to human beings which are the most complex, and, therefore, the most evolved Life forms upon our planet. We were taught, in other words, that evolution means the progressive development of organizational complexity.

This definition is an expression of the idea that the organism that is best able to control both its environment

3

and all of the other organisms in its environment is the most evolved. "Survival of the fittest" means that the most evolved organism in a given environment is the organism that is at the top of the food chain in that environment. According to this definition, therefore, the organism that is most able to ensure its own survival, most able to serve its self-preservation, is the most evolved.

We have long known that this definition of evolution is inadequate, but we have not known why. When two humans engage one another, they are, in terms of organizational complexity, equally evolved. If both have the same intelligence, yet one is small-minded, mean, and selfish while the other is magnanimous and altruistic, we say that the one who is magnanimous and altruistic is the more evolved. If one human intentionally sacrifices his or her life to save another, by, for example, using his or her own body to shield another from a bullet or a speeding car, we say that the human who sacrificed his or her life, indeed, was one of the most evolved among us. We know these things to be true, but they are at variance with our understanding of evolution.

Jesus, we are told, foresaw the plot against His life, even to the details of how His friends would act and react, yet He did not run from what He saw. The entirety of humankind has been inexorably shaped by the power and love of One who *gave His life* for others. All who revere Him, and almost all who but know His story, agree that He was one of the most evolved of our species.

Our deeper understanding tells us that a truly evolved

being is one that values others more than it values itself, and that values love more than it values the physical world and what is in it. We must now bring our understanding of evolution into alignment with this deeper understanding. It is important that we do this because our current understanding of evolution reflects the phase of evolution that we are now leaving. By examining this understanding, we can perceive how we have evolved to now, and what we are now in the process of leaving behind. By reflecting upon a new and expanded understanding of evolution, one that validates our deepest truths, we can see what we are evolving into, and what that means in terms of what we experience, what we value, and how we act.

Our current understanding of evolution results from the fact that we have evolved until now by exploring physical reality with our five senses. We have been, until now, five-sensory human beings. This path of evolution has allowed us to see the basic principles of the Universe in concrete ways. We see through our five senses that every action is a cause that has an effect, and that every effect has a cause. We see the results of our intentions. We see that rage kills: It takes away breath—the Life force—and it spills blood—the carrier of vitality. We see that kindness nurtures. We see and feel the effects of a snarl and a smile.

We experience our ability to process knowledge. We see, for example, that a stick is a tool, and we see the effects of how we choose to use it. The club that kills can drive a stake into the ground to hold a shelter. The spear that takes a life can be used as a lever to ease life's burdens. The knife that cuts flesh can be used to cut cloth. The hands that build bombs can be used to build schools. The minds that coordinate the activities of violence can coordinate the activities of cooperation.

We see that when the activities of life are infused with reverence, they come alive with meaning and purpose. We see that when reverence is lacking from life's activities, the result is cruelty, violence, and loneliness. The physical arena is a magnificent learning environment. It is a school within which, through experimentation, we come to understand what causes us to expand and what causes us to contract, what causes us to grow and what causes us to shrivel, what nourishes our souls and what depletes them, what works and what does not.

When the physical environment is seen only from the five-sensory point of view, physical survival appears to be the fundamental criterion of evolution because no other kind of evolution is detectable. It is from this point of view that "survival of the fittest" appears to be synonymous with evolution, and physical dominance appears to characterize advanced evolution.

When perception of the physical world is limited to the five-sensory modality, the basis of life in the physical arena becomes fear. Power to control the environment, and those within the environment appears to be essential.

The need for physical dominance produces a type of competition that affects every aspect of our lives. It affects relationships between lovers and between superpowers, between siblings and between races, between classes and between sexes. It disrupts the natural tendency toward harmony between nations and between friends. The same energy that sent warships to the Persian Gulf sent soldiers to Vietnam and Crusaders to Palestine. The energy that separated the family of Romeo from the family of Juliet is the same energy that separates the racial family of the black husband from the racial family of the white wife. The energy that set Lee Harvey Oswald against John Kennedy is the same energy that set Cain against Abel. Brothers and sisters quarrel for the same reason that corporations quarrel—they seek power over one another.

The power to control the environment, and those within it, is power over what can be felt, smelled, tasted, heard, or seen. This type of power is external power. External power can be acquired or lost, as in the stock market or an election. It can be bought or stolen, transferred or inherited. It is thought of as something that can be gotten from someone else, or somewhere else. One person's gain of external power is perceived as another person's loss. The result of seeing power as external is violence and destruction. All of our institutions—social, economic, and political—reflect our understanding of power as external.

Families, like cultures, are patriarchal or matriarchal. One person "wears the pants." Children learn this early, and it shapes their lives.

Police departments, like the military, are produced by the

perception of power as external. Badge, boots, rank, radio, uniform, weapons, and armor are symbols of fear. Those who wear them are fearful. They fear to engage the world without defenses. Those who encounter these symbols are fearful. They fear the power that these symbols represent, or they fear those whom they expect this power to contain, or they fear both. The police and the military, like patriarchal and matriarchal families and cultures, are not origins of the perception of power as external. They are reflections of the way that we, as a species and as individuals, have come to view power.

The perception of power as external has shaped our economics. The ability to control economies, within communities and within nations, and the ability to control the transnational economy of the world, is concentrated in the hands of a few people. To protect workers from these people, we have created unions. To protect consumers, we have created bureaucracies in government. To protect the poor, we have created welfare systems. This is a perfect reflection of how we have come to perceive power—as the possession of a few while the majority serve it as victims.

Money is a symbol of external power. Those who have the most money have the most ability to control their environment and those within it, while those who have the least money have the least ability to control their environment and those within it. Money is acquired, lost, stolen, inherited, and fought for. Education, social status, fame, and things that are owned, if we derive a sense of increased security from them, are symbols of external power. Anything we fear to lose—a home, a car, an attractive body, an agile mind, a deep belief—is a symbol of external power. What we fear is an increase in our vulnerability. This results from seeing power as external.

When power is seen as external, the hierarchies of our social, economic, and political structures, as well as the hierarchies of the Universe, appear as indicators of who has power and who does not. Those at the top appear to have the most power and, therefore, to be the most valuable and the least vulnerable. Those at the bottom appear to be the least powerful, and, therefore, to be the least valuable and the most vulnerable. From this perception, the general is more valuable than the private, the executive is more valuable than the chauffeur, the doctor is more valuable than the receptionist, the parent is more valuable than the child, and the Divine is more valuable than the worshiper. We fear to transgress our parents, our bosses, and our God. All perceptions of lesser and greater personal value result from the perception of power as external.

Competition for external power lies at the heart of all violence. The secondary gain behind ideological conflicts, such as capitalism versus communism, and religious conflicts, such as Irish Catholic versus Irish Protestant, and geographical conflicts, such as Jew versus Arab, and familial and marital conflicts, is external power.

The perception of power as external splinters the psyche, whether it is the psyche of the individual, the community, the nation, or the world. There is no difference between acute schizophrenia and a world at war. There is no difference between the agony of a splintered soul and the agony of a splintered nation. When a husband and a wife compete for power, they engage the same dynamic that humans of one race do when they fear humans of another race.

From these dynamics, we have formed our present understanding of evolution as a process of ever-increasing ability to dominate the environment and each other. This definition reflects the limitations of perceiving the physical world with only five senses. It reflects the competition for external power that is generated by fear.

After millennia of brutality to one another, individual to individual and group to group, it is now clear that the insecurity which underlies the perception of power as external cannot be healed by the accumulation of external power. It is evident for all to see, not only with each newscast and evening paper, but also through each of our countless sufferings as individuals and as a species, that the perception of power as external brings only pain, violence, and destruction. This is how we have evolved until now, and this is what we are leaving behind.

Our deeper understanding leads us to another kind of power, a power that loves life in every form that it appears, a power that does not judge what it encounters, a power that perceives meaningfulness and purpose in the smallest details upon the Earth. This is authentic power. When we align our thoughts, emotions, and actions with the highest part of ourselves, we are filled with enthusiasm, purpose, and meaning. Life is rich and full. We have no thoughts of bitterness. We have no memory of fear. We are joyously and intimately engaged with our world. This is the experience of authentic power.

Authentic power has its roots in the deepest source of our being. Authentic power cannot be bought, inherited, or hoarded. An authentically empowered person is incapable of making anyone or anything a victim. An authentically empowered person is one who is so strong, so empowered, that the idea of using force against another is not a part of his or her consciousness.

No understanding of evolution is adequate that does not have at its core that we are on a journey toward authentic power, and that authentic empowerment is the goal of our evolutionary process and the purpose of our being. We are evolving from a species that pursues external power into a species that pursues authentic power. We are leaving behind exploration of the physical world as our sole means of evolution. This means of evolution, and the consciousness that results from an awareness that is limited to the five-sensory modality, are no longer adequate to what we must become.

We are evolving from five-sensory humans into multi-sensory humans. Our five senses, together, form a single sensory system that is designed to perceive physical reality. The perceptions of a multisensory human extend beyond physical reality to the larger dynamical systems of which our physical reality is a part. The multisensory human is able to perceive, and to appreciate, the role that our physical reality plays in a larger picture of evolution, and the dynamics by which our physical reality is created and sustained. This realm is invisible to the five-sensory human.

It is in this invisible realm that the origins of our deepest values are found. From the perspective of this invisible realm, the motivations of those who consciously sacrifice their lives for higher purposes make sense, the power of Gandhi is explicable, and the compassionate acts of the Christ are comprehensible in a fullness that is not accessible to the five-sensory human.

All of our great teachers have been, or are, multisensory humans. They have spoken to us and acted in accordance with perceptions and values that reflect the larger perspective of the multisensory being, and, therefore, their words and actions awaken within us the recognition of truths.

From the perception of the five-sensory human, we are alone in a universe that is physical. From the perception of the multisensory human, we are never alone, and the Universe is alive, conscious, intelligent, and compassionate. From the perception of the five-sensory human, the physical world is an unaccountable given in which we unaccountably find ourselves, and we strive to dominate it so that we can survive. From the perception of the multisensory human, the physical world is a learning environment that is created jointly by the souls that share it, and everything that occurs within it serves their learning. From the perception of the five-sensory human, intentions have no effects, the effects of actions are physical, and not all actions affect us or others. From the perception of the multisensory human, the intention behind an action determines its effects, every intention affects both us and others, and the effects of intentions extend far beyond the physical world.

What does it mean to say that an "invisible" realm exists in which the origins of our deeper understandings are located? What are the implications of considering the existence of a realm that is not detectable through the five senses, but that can be known, explored, and understood by other human faculties?

When a question is asked that cannot be answered within the common frame of reference, it can be classified as nonsensical, or it can be dismissed as a question that is not appropriate, or the person who is asking the question can expand his or her consciousness to encompass a frame of reference from which the question can be answered. The first two options are the easy ways out of a confrontation with a question that appears to be nonsensical or inappropriate, but the seeker, the true scientist, will allow himself or herself to expand into a frame of reference from which the answers that he or she is seeking can be understood.

We, as a species, have been asking the questions "Is there a God?", "Is there a Divine Intelligence?", and "Is there a purpose to life?" for as long as we have been able to articulate questions. The time has now come for us to expand into a frame of reference that allows these questions to be answered.

The larger frame of reference of the multisensory human allows an understanding of the experientially meaningful distinction between the personality and the soul. Your personality is that part of you that was born into, lives within, and will die within time. To be a human and to have a personality are the same thing. Your personality, like your body, is the vehicle of your evolution.

The decisions that you make and the actions that you take upon the Earth are the means by which you evolve. At each moment you choose the intentions that will shape your experiences and those things upon which you will focus your attention. These choices affect your evolutionary process. This is so for each person. If you choose unconsciously, you evolve unconsciously. If you choose consciously, you evolve consciously.

The fearful and violent emotions that have come to characterize human existence can be experienced only by the personality. Only the personality can feel anger, fear, hatred, vengeance, sorrow, shame, regret, indifference, frustration, cynicism, and loneliness. Only the personality can judge, manipulate and exploit. Only the personality can pursue external power. The personality can also be loving, compassionate, and wise in its relations with others, but love, compassion, and wisdom do not come from the personality. They are experiences of the soul.

Your soul is that part of you that is immortal. Every person has a soul, but a personality that is limited in its perception to the five senses is not aware of its soul, and, therefore, cannot recognize the influences of its soul. As a personality becomes multisensory, its intuitions—its hunches and subtle feelings—become important to it. It senses things about itself, other people, and the situations in which it finds itself that it cannot justify on the basis of the information that its five senses can provide. It comes to recognize intentions, and to respond to them rather than to the actions and the words that it encounters. It can recognize, for example, a warm heart beneath a harsh and angry manner, and a cold heart beneath polished and pleasing words.

When a multisensory personality looks inside itself, it finds a multitude of different currents. Through experience, it learns to distinguish between these currents and to identify the emotional, psychological, and physical effects of each. It learns, for example, which currents produce anger, divisive thoughts, and destructive actions, and which currents produce love, healing thoughts, and constructive actions. In time, it learns to value and to identify with those currents that generate creativity, healing, and love, and to challenge and release those currents that create negativity, disharmony, and violence. In this way, a personality comes to experience the energy of its soul.

Your soul is not a passive or a theoretical entity that occupies a space in the vicinity of your chest cavity. It is a positive, purposeful force at the core of your being. It is that part of you that understands the impersonal nature of the energy dynamics in which you are involved, that loves without restriction and accepts without judgment.

If you desire to know your soul, the first step is to recognize that you have a soul. The next step is to allow yourself to consider, "If I have a soul, what *is* my soul? What does my soul want? What is the relationship between my soul and me? How does my soul affect my life?"

When the energy of the soul is recognized, acknowledged, and valued, it begins to infuse the life of the personality. When the personality comes fully to serve the energy of its soul, that is authentic empowerment. This is the goal of the evolutionary process in which we are involved and the reason for our being. Every experience that you have and will have upon the Earth encourages the alignment of your personality with your soul. Every circumstance and situation gives you the opportunity to choose this path, to allow your soul to shine through you, to bring into the physical world through you its unending and unfathomable reverence for and love of Life.

This is a book about authentic empowerment—the alignment of the personality with the soul—what that involves, how it happens, and what it creates. To understand these things requires an understanding of things that appear unusual to the five-sensory human, but they become natural once you understand evolution—that five-sensory perception is a journey leading to multisensory perception—and that you were not always meant to be five-sensory.*

---

* To learn how to apply what you have learned in this chapter and deepen your experiences, see the Chapter 1 Study Guide on page 245.

2

Karma

Most of us are accustomed to the belief that our participation in the process of evolution is limited to the duration of a single lifetime. This belief reflects the perspective of the five-sensory personality. From the point of view of the five-sensory personality, nothing of itself lasts beyond its lifetime, and there is nothing in the experience of the five-sensory human that is not of itself. The multisensory human, too, understands that nothing of itself lasts beyond its lifetime, but it is also aware of its immortal soul.

The lifetime of your personality is one of a myriad of experiences of your soul. The soul exists outside of time. The perspective of the soul is immense, and the perception of the soul is without the limitations of the personality. Souls that have chosen the physical experience of life as we know it as a path of evolution, have, in general, incarnated their energies many times into many psychological and physical forms. For each incarnation, the soul creates a different personality and body. The personality and the body that, for the five-sensory human, are the experiential entirety of its existence, are, for its soul, the unique and perfectly suited instruments of a particular incarnation.

Each personality contributes, in its own special way, with its own special aptitudes and lessons to learn, consciously or unconsciously, to the evolution of its soul. The life of a mother, a warrior, a daughter, a priest; the experiences of love, vulnerability, fear, loss, and tenderness; the struggles with anger, defiance, emptiness, and jealousy—all serve the evolution of the soul. Each physical, emotional, and psychological characteristic that comprises a personality and its body—strong or weak arms, dense or penetrating intellect, happy or despairing disposition, yellow or black skin, even hair and eye color—is perfectly suited to its soul's purpose.

The five-sensory personality is not aware of the many other incarnations of its soul. A multisensory personality may be conscious of these incarnations, or experience them, as its own past or future lives. They are in its family of lives, so to speak, but they are not lives that it, itself, has lived. They are experiences of its soul.

From the point of view of the soul, all of its incarnations are simultaneous. All of its personalities exist at once. Therefore, the release of negativity that occurs in one of the soul's incarnations benefits not only itself, but all of its soul's other incarnations also. Because the soul, itself, is not confined to time, the past of a personality, as well as its future, is enhanced when a personality releases currents of fear and doubt. As we shall see, the release of negativity by a personality benefits a great many other dynamics of consciousness as well. Some of these can be perceived by the five-sensory human, but appear to him or her neither as dynamics of consciousness, nor as related to his or her inner processes, such as the consciousness and evolution of his or her sex, race, nation, and culture. Others extend far beyond the perceptual ability of the five-sensory human. A conscious lifetime, therefore, is a treasure beyond value.

The personality and its body are artificial aspects of the soul. When they have served their functions, at the end of the soul's incarnation, the soul releases them. They come to an end, but the soul does not. After an incarnation, the soul returns to its immortal and timeless state. It returns once again to its natural state of compassion, clarity, and boundless love.

This is the context in which our evolution occurs: the continual incarnation and reincarnation of the energy of the soul into the physical arena, into our Earth school.

Why does this happen? Why is it necessary even to speak of personalities and souls?

The incarnation of a soul is a massive reduction of the power of the soul to a scale that is appropriate to a physical form. It is a reduction of an immortal Life system into the framework of time and the span of a few years. It is the reduction of a perceptual system that partakes simultaneously, through direct experience, of countless lifetimes, some of them physical and some of them nonphysical, to the five physical senses. The soul chooses, voluntarily, to undertake this experience in order to heal.

The personality is those parts of the soul that require healing, along with those parts of the soul, such as compassion and love, that the soul has lent to the process of healing in that lifetime. The splintered aspects of the soul, the aspects that require healing, need to interact in physical matter so that each part of the splinteredness can become whole. The personality is like a complex mandala that is formed from these splintered parts in addition to the parts that are not splintered. It comes directly from the parts of the soul that the soul has chosen to work on in this lifetime to heal, that need to experience physical matter, and those parts that the soul has given to the process of healing in which you are involved. Therefore, you can see within a person's personality the splintered suffering of the soul from which it was formed, as well as the grace that the soul has earned, which is the loving part of the personality.

Consider how powerful the soul is if it can have a part of itself that experiences great love, a part of itself that experiences fears, a part that is perhaps neutral, a part that experiences schizophrenia, and a part that is dramatically compassionate. If any of these parts are incomplete, the personality that the soul forms will be out of harmony. The harmonious personality is one in which the soul flows easily through the part of itself that is in touch with its physical incarnation.

The soul is. It has no beginning and no end but flows toward wholeness. The personality emerges as a natural force from the soul. It is an energy tool that the soul adapts to function within the physical world. Each personality is unique because the configuration of energy of the soul that formed it is unique. It is the persona of the soul, so to speak, that interacts with physical matter. It is a product that is formed from the vibrational aspect of your name, the vibrational aspect of your relationship to planets at the time of your incarnation, and vibrational aspects of your energy environment, as well as from the splintered aspects of your soul that need to interact in physical matter in order to be brought into wholeness.

The personality does not operate independently from the soul. To the extent that a person is in touch with spiritual depths, the personality is soothed because the energy of consciousness is focused on its energy core and not on its artificial facade, which is the personality.

The personality sometimes appears as a force running rampant in the world with no attachment to the energy of its soul. This situation can be the origin of what we call an evil human being, and it can be the origin of a schizophrenic human being. It is the result of the personality being unable to find its reference point, or connection, to its mothership, which is its soul. The conflicts of a human's life are directly proportional to the distance at which an energy of personality exists separately from the soul, and, therefore, as we shall see, in an irresponsible position of creation. When a personality is in full balance, you cannot see where it ends and the soul begins. That is a whole human being.

What is involved in the healing of a soul?

Most of us are accustomed to the idea that we are responsible for some of our actions, but not all of them. We consider ourselves responsible, for example, for the good deed that brings our neighbor and us together, or for responding to it positively, but we do not consider ourselves responsible for the argument between us and our neighbor, or for responding to it negatively. We consider ourselves responsible for having a safe trip if we take the time to check the condition of the car before starting, but if we speed around a car that, in our opinion, has been traveling too slowly, and almost cause an accident by doing that, we consider the other driver to be responsible. If we feed and clothe ourselves through our successful business, we credit ourselves. If we feed and clothe ourselves by burglarizing apartments, we blame our difficult childhood.

For many of us, being held responsible is equal to getting caught. A friend who returns each year to his native Italy told me, with a twinkle in his eye, of a dinner out with his family. When the bill came, my friend's father, who is fastidious, examined each scribbled item. After some study, he deciphered the last entry and recognized it to be a short expression that translates, roughly, "If it goes, it goes." He called the waiter and asked, "What is this item?" The waiter shrugged, "It didn't go." Many of us feel that if a clerk gives us too much change, and we take it, our life has been affected only to the extent that we have come into an unexpected gain. In fact, each of our acts affects us in far-reaching ways.

Every action, thought, and feeling is motivated by an intention, and that intention is a cause that exists as one with an effect. If we participate in the cause, it is not possible for us not to participate in the effect. In this most profound way, we are held responsible for our every action, thought, and feeling, which is to say, for our every intention. We, ourselves, shall partake of the fruit of our every intention. It is, therefore, wise for us to become aware of the many intentions that inform our experience, to sort out which intentions produce which effects, and to choose our intentions according to the effects that we desire to produce.

This is the way that we learned about physical reality as children, and that we refine our knowledge of it as adults. We learn the effect of crying when we are hungry, and we repeat the cause that brings us the effect that we desire. We learn the effect of putting a finger in a light socket, and we do not repeat the cause that produces that effect.

We also learn about intentions and their effects through our experiences in physical reality, but learning that intentions produce specific effects, and what those effects are, proceeds slowly when our learning must be done solely through the density of physical matter. Anger, for example, causes distance and hostile interactions. If we must learn this solely through physical experience, we may have to experience ten, or fifty, or one hundred and fifty circumstances of distance from another and hostile interaction before we come to understand that it is the orientation of anger on our part, the intention of hostility and distance, and not this particular action or that, which produces the effect that we do not want. This is predominantly the way that a five-sensory human learns.

The relationship of cause and effect within the domain of physical objects and phenomena reflects a dynamic that is not limited to physical reality. This is the dynamic of karma. Everything in the physical world, including each of us, is a small part of dynamics that are more extensive than a five-sensory human can perceive. The love, fear, compassion, and anger that you experience, for example, are only a small part of the love, fear, compassion, and anger of a larger energy system that you do not see.

Within physical reality, the dynamic of karma is reflected by the third law of motion: "For every action there is an equal and opposite reaction." In other words, the great law of karma that governs the balancing of energy within our evolutionary system is reflected within the domain of physical objects and phenomena by the last of three principles, three laws of motion, that govern the balancing of energy within physical reality.

The law of karma is an impersonal energy dynamic. When its effects are personalized, that is, experienced from the point of view of the personality, they are experienced as a reversal in the direction, a coming back to the intender, of the energy of his or her intention. This is how the personality experiences the impersonal dynamic that is described by the third law as an "equal and opposite reaction." The person who intends hatred for others experiences the intention of hatred from others. The person who intends love for others experiences the intention of love from others, and so forth. The Golden Rule is a behavioral guide that is based upon the dynamic of karma. A personalized statement of karma would be, "You receive from the world what you give to the world."

Karma is not a moral dynamic. Morality is a human creation. The Universe does not judge. The law of karma governs the balancing of energy within our system of morality and within those of our neighbors. It serves humanity as an impersonal and Universal teacher of responsibility.

Every cause that has not yet produced its effect is an event that has not yet come to completion. It is an imbalance of energy that is in the process of becoming balanced. That balancing of energy does not always occur within the span of a single lifetime. The karma of your soul is created and balanced by the activities of its many personalities, including you. Often a personality experiences effects that were created by other of its soul's personalities, and, conversely, creates energy imbalances that are not able to right themselves within its own lifetime. Therefore, without knowledge of its soul, reincarnation, and karma, it is not always possible for a personality to understand the significance or the meaning of the events of its life, or to understand the effects of its responses to them.

For example, a personality that takes advantage of others creates an imbalance of energy that must be righted by the experience of being taken advantage of by others. If that cannot be accomplished within the lifetime of this personality, another of its soul's personalities will experience being taken advantage of by other people. If that personality does not understand that the experience of being taken advantage of by others is the effect of a previous cause, and that this experience is bringing to completion an impersonal process, it will react from a personal point of view rather than from the point of view of its soul. It may become angry, for example, or vengeful or depressed. It may lash out, or grow cynical or withdraw into sorrow. Each of these responses creates karma, another imbalance of energy which, in turn, must be balanced. In this way, one karmic debt has been paid, so to speak, but another, or others, has been created.

If a child dies early in its life, we do not know what agreement was made between that child's soul and the souls of its parents, or what healing was served by that experience. Although we are sympathetic to the anguish of the parents, we cannot judge this event. If we, or the parents of this child, do not understand the impersonal nature of the dynamic that is in motion, we may react with anger toward the Universe, or toward each other, or with guilt if we feel that our actions were inadequate. All of these reactions create karma, and more lessons for the soul to learn—more karmic debts for the soul to pay—appear.

In order to become whole, the soul must balance its energy. It must experience the effects that it has caused. The energy imbalances in the soul are the incomplete parts of the soul that form the personality. Personalities in interaction are souls that are seeking to heal. Whether an interaction between souls is healing or not depends upon whether the personality involved can see beyond itself and that of the other personality to the interaction of their souls. This perception automatically draws forth compassion. Every experience, and every interaction, provides you with an opportunity to look from the point of view of your soul or from the point of view of your personality.

What does this mean in practical terms? How does a personality begin to look beyond itself and to see its soul in interaction with the souls of others?

Since we cannot know what is being healed through each interaction—what karmic debts are coming to conclusion—we cannot judge what we see. For example, when we see a person sleeping in the gutter in the winter, we do not know what is being completed for that soul. We do not know whether that soul has engaged in cruelty in another lifetime, and now has chosen to experience the same dynamic from an entirely different point of view, as, for example, the recipient of charity. It is appropriate that we respond to his or her circumstance with compassion, but it is not appropriate that we perceive it as unfair, because it is not.

There are personalities that are selfish and hostile and negative, but even in these cases we cannot fully know the reasons why. These are hidden from view. That does not mean that we cannot recognize negativity when we see it, but we cannot judge it. That is not our place. If we intervene in an argument, or break up a fight, it is not appropriate that we judge the participants. Of one thing we can be certain: A person that is engaging in violence is hurting deeply, because a healthy and balanced soul is incapable of harming another.

When we judge, we create negative karma. Judgment is a function of the personality. When we say of another soul, "She is worthy," or, "He is not worthy," we create negative karma. When we say of an action, "This is right," or, "That is wrong," we create negative karma. This does not mean that we should not act appropriately to the circumstances in which we find ourselves.

If our car is hit by another car, for example, and the driver of the other car is drunk, it is appropriate that the other driver be held responsible, through the courts, for the repair of our car. It is appropriate that he or she be prohibited from driving while intoxicated. It is not appropriate that we allow our actions to be motivated by feelings of indignation, righteousness, or victimization. These feelings are the result of judgments that we make about ourselves and the other person, assessments through which we see ourselves as superior to another being.

If we act upon these feelings, not only do we increase the karmic obligations of our soul, but we also are not able to enter into these feelings and learn from them. Feelings, as we shall see, are the means through which we can discern the parts of itself that the soul seeks to heal, and through which we come to see the action of the soul in physical matter. The road to your soul is through your heart.

If we are to engage the viewpoint of the soul, we must cease from judging, even those events that appear to be unfathomable, such as the cruelty of an inquisition or a holocaust, the death of an infant, the prolonged agony of a death by cancer, or a life confined to a bed. We do not know what is being healed in these sufferings, or the details of the energetic circumstance that is coming into balance. It is appropriate that we allow ourselves to feel the compassion that such circumstances call forth in us and to act upon it, but if we allow ourselves to judge these events and those who participate in them, we create negative karma that must be balanced, and we, ourselves, will be among those souls that choose to participate in circumstances that are necessary to that balancing.

If we do not judge, how can there be justice?

Gandhi was beaten several times during his life. Although on two occasions he nearly died, he refused to prosecute his attackers because he saw that they were doing "what they thought was right." This position of non-judgmental acceptance was central in Gandhi's life. The Christ did not judge even those who spit in His face, and who subjected Him without mercy to His pain and humiliation. He asked forgiveness, not vengeance, for those who tortured Him. Did neither the Christ nor Gandhi know the meaning of justice?

They knew non-judgmental justice.

What is non-judgmental justice?

Non-judgmental justice is a perception that allows you to see everything in life, but does not engage your negative emotions. Non-judgmental justice relieves you of the self-appointed job of judge and jury because you know that everything is being seen—nothing escapes the law of karma—and this brings forth understanding and compassion. Non-judgmental justice is the freedom of seeing what you see and experiencing what you experience without responding negatively. It allows you to experience directly the unobstructed flow of the intelligence, radiance, and love of the Universe of which our physical reality is a part. Non-judgmental justice flows naturally from understanding the soul and how it evolves.

This, then, is the framework of our evolutionary process: the continual incarnation and reincarnation of the energy of the soul into physical reality for the purposes of healing and balancing its energy in accordance with the law of karma. Within this framework we evolve, as individuals and as a species, through the cycle of being unempowered to becoming empowered, yet the experiences that we encounter in this process need not be the kind that we have encountered to now.*

---

* To learn how to apply what you have learned in this chapter and deepen your experiences, see the Chapter 2 Study Guide on page 251.

3

Reverence

The framework of karma and reincarnation in which we evolve is neutral. Actions and reactions in the physical arena set energy into motion, forming our experiences and revealing in the process the lessons that the soul has yet to learn. When our actions create discord in another person, we, ourselves, in this lifetime or in another, will feel that discord. Likewise, if our actions create harmony and empowerment in another, we also will come to feel that harmony and empowerment. This allows us to experience the effects of what we have created, and thereby to learn to create responsibly.

The framework of karma and reincarnation is impersonal, and provides for each soul, in response to the actions of its personalities, the experiences that it requires in order to evolve. Therefore, the orientation, or the attitude, with which a personality approaches the evolutionary process determines the nature of the experiences that will be required for the evolution of its soul. An angry personality, for example, will respond to the difficulties of its life with anger, and thereby bring into being the necessity of experiencing the results of anger; a sorrowful personality will respond sorrowfully and bring into being the necessity of experiencing the results of sorrow, and so on.

A person who is angry, and yet reveres Life, however, will respond very differently to the difficulties of his or her life than a person who is angry and has no reverence for Life. The person who has no reverence for Life will not hesitate to strike out against Life. The violence that is released in killing another person, or another living creature, is much greater than the violence that is released in speaking angry words. The karmic obligation—the energy imbalance—that is created by killing can be balanced only by the experience of a commensurate brutality. Thus, a person who is reverent will automatically be spared the severe karmic consequences of one who is not.

Even if all of our species were reverent, that would not end the need for us to move through our own evolution. It would just change the quality of the learnings within the process of evolution. In other words, if we became reverent this day, we would not be exempt from the demands of our evolution, but the quality of the experiences that we would encounter would be different. We would not harm Life. We would still learn the same thing, but in the process of learning, we would not seek to harm or to destroy. Our journey from powerlessness to authentic empowerment would continue, but the nature of that experience would change. We would not encounter the types of experiences that result from a perception of the world that lacks reverence.

We see Life as cheap. This perception pervades all of our perceptions. When we look at the animal kingdom, for example, we see the activities within this kingdom as verification of our evaluation of Life. We see animals kill and feed upon other animals, and we conclude that weaker forms of Life exist only to nourish the stronger. We justify our exploitation of Life upon what we perceive to be the design of Nature. We maim and kill. We create situations in which millions of people starve while we store grain in silos and pour milk down drains. We look upon each other as prey to satisfy our emotional and physical needs. We say, "It's a dog-eat-dog world," and that to survive in it we must take advantage of others before they take advantage of us. We look upon Life as a contest that produces winners and losers, and we feel no restraints upon us when the needs of other people or other groups threaten us.

Our behavior and values are so much shaped by perceptions that lack reverence that we do not know what it is like to be reverent. When we curse a competitor or strive to disempower another person, we absent ourselves from reverence. When we work to take instead of to give, we labor without reverence. When we strive for safety at the expense of another person's safety, we deprive ourselves of the protection of reverence. When we judge one person as superior and another as inferior we depart from reverence. When we judge ourselves, we do the same thing. Business, politics, education, sex, raising families, and personal interactions without reverence all produce the same result: human beings using other human beings.

Our species has become arrogant. We behave as though the Earth were ours to do with as we please. We pollute its land, oceans, and atmosphere to satisfy our needs without thinking of the needs of the other life forms that live upon the Earth, or of the needs of the Earth. We believe that we are conscious and that the Universe is not. We think and act as though our existence as living forces in the Universe will end with this lifetime, and that we are responsible neither to others nor to the Universe.

It is not possible for a reverent person to exploit his or her friends, co-workers, city, nation, or planet. It is not possible for a reverent species to create caste systems, child labor, nerve gas, or nuclear weapons. Therefore, it is not possible for a reverent person, or a reverent species, to accumulate the type of karma that such activities create.

Why is this? What is reverence?

Reverence is engaging in a form and a depth of contact with Life that is well beyond the shell of form and into essence. Reverence is contact with the essence of each thing and person and plant and bird and animal. It is contact with the interior of its beingness. Even if you cannot sense the interior, it is enough to know that the form, the shell, is merely an outer layer, and that underneath it the true power and essence of who a person is, or what a thing is, is present. That is what is honored in reverence.

Process is honored in reverence. The unfolding of Life, the maturation process, the process of growing through and coming into your own empowerment, is a process that needs to be approached with reverence.

The cycles of Life need to be approached with reverence. They have been in place for billions of years. They are the reflection of the natural breathing of the soul of Gaia itself, the Earth consciousness, as it moves its force fields and guides the cycles of Life. If these are revered, how could we look at something as exquisite as our Earth's ecology and do one thing that would risk the balance of this system?

Reverence is an attitude of honoring Life. You do not have to be authentically empowered to be gentle with Life or to love Life. There are many people who are not authentically empowered but who are quite reverent. They would harm nothing. Often it is the case that they are the most compassionate and the most loving people because they have suffered so much.

Whether a person is reverent depends essentially upon whether he or she accepts the principle of the sacredness of Life, any way that he or she defines sacred.

Reverence is also simply the experience of accepting that all Life is, in and of itself, of value.

Reverence is not respect. Respect is a judgment. It is a

response to the perception of qualities that we ourselves admire, or have been taught to admire. Qualities that are admired by the people of one culture may not be admired by the people of another culture, or by the people of a subculture, or by another generation of the same culture. Therefore, what is respected by some people may not be respected by others. It is possible to respect one person and not respect another, but it is not possible to revere one person without revering every person.

Reverence is a perception, but it is a holy perception. The perception of holiness is not one that we use continually. It is one that we apply to religion, but not to the process of evolution or the learning process of the human Life, and so we do not approach the need to learn and all of the learning experiences of our lives with regard for their purpose against the background of spiritual development. Perceiving in this way is true reverence, because it allows you to look at what you are going through and to see it within the framework of the evolution and the maturation of your own spirit. It is true reverence, because it enables you to look at all the evolutions that are taking place simultaneously with your own, in all of the kingdoms of Life, and fully appreciate, or at least see very differently, how they unfold.

Only when we see through eyes that lack reverence, for example, does the feeding of one animal upon another appear to be a cruel system instead of one where species learn to give to each other, where there is a natural give and take and sharing of the energies between kingdoms. This is ecology: the natural redistribution of energy between kingdoms.

It is only our kingdom, the human kingdom, that wants to warehouse energy, to use much more than it needs and to store what it does not, so that the balance of the cycle is disturbed so dramatically. If each of us took only what he or she needed for that day, it would be perfect. Animals do not warehouse like us, except in the case of animals that need to for winter.

The perception of reverence allows us to see the interdependency of different species from a more comprehensive and compassionate perspective. It allows us to see the significance of each living creature, and its experiences, to the compassionate unfolding of the Universe. This perspective is much less likely to create violent or destructive responses within us as we grow through our lives because it reveals in each moment the value of all Life.

Approaching and regarding Life with an attitude of reverence permits the experience of being unempowered but not cruel. As you work toward becoming reverent, your tendencies toward harming others and other forms of Life diminish. As you acquire a sense of reverence, you develop a capacity to think more deeply about the value of Life before you commit your energy to action. When you are fully reverent, you cannot harm Life, even though you are unempowered. Without reverence the experience of being unempowered can become a very cruel one because a disempowered person is a frightened person, and if a frightened person has no sense of reverence, he or she will harm or kill indiscriminately.

Reverence is a level of protection and honor about the

process of life so that while a person is maturing toward the journey and through the journey of authentic empowerment, he or she harms nothing. Because we have no reverence, our journey to empowerment often includes the experiences of victimizing life. Therefore, there are victims and victimizers. The process of destroying Life while we are learning about Life that has characterized our evolution would cease, or at least would be very different, if we approached Life with a quality of reverence.

It is because we have no sense of reverence, no true belief in the holiness of all Life, that Life is destroyed and tortured, brutalized, starved, and maimed while we journey from unempowerment to empowerment. If a sense of reverence were brought into the process of evolution, then as each of us, and our species, moves through the cycle of being unempowered to becoming empowered, the many learnings that are contained within that growing process of evolution would not likely produce violence and fear to the extent that it is now experienced.

The destructions of human Life, plant Life, animal Life, and the planet would be considerably diminished, or would cease, if there were an active principle of reverence within our species, if there were the perception within our species, and within each of us, that although we are engaged in evolutionary processes that require personal learning, that does not authorize us to destroy Life while we are learning, or because we are. We would not have the karmic energy of destruction, only of learning. Even though learning is contained in destruction, the karmic consequences of participating in violence and destruction are a high price to pay for it.

It is not necessary, in other words, to learn what we need to learn and have it cost somebody his or her life. It is not necessary for progress and the experience of progress to cost the destruction of nature. It is not necessary, but without a sense of reverence for Life, who cares that it destroys Life? Without reverence, Life becomes a very cheap commodity, as it is upon our planet now where the entire process and the sacredness of evolution is not regarded, accepted, or honored.

If we perceived Life with reverence, and understood our evolutionary process, we would stand in awe at the experience of physical Life and walk the Earth in a very deep sense of gratitude. As it is, there are billions of human beings who are filled with regret that they are on the Earth, with overwhelming experiences of pain, despair, discouragement, depression, starvation, and disease. These are the things of our planet. They result largely from the fact that so much of the human condition is without reverence.

Reverence is a perception of the soul. Only the personality can perceive Life without reverence. Reverence is a natural aspect of authentic empowerment because the soul reveres all of Life. Therefore, when the personality is aligned with the soul, it cannot perceive Life except with reverence. Approaching Life with reverence not only protects the soul from the karmic obligations that are created by personalities that do not honor Life, but it also is a step toward moving the personality into alignment with the soul because it brings an aspect of the soul directly into the physical environment.

What does the decision to approach Life with reverence mean in practical terms?

It means challenging the perceptions and the values of a five-sensory world that lacks reverence. This is not always easy, especially for males who have been taught values that serve the accumulation of external power. An authentically empowered male will not be embarrassed or feel less than fully masculine by showing concern for Life, and for the many creatures on our planet. That is very much the energy of reverence. Therefore, the decision to approach Life with reverence often requires courage, not only of men, but also of women who have adopted these values.

The decision to become a reverent person is essentially the decision to become a spiritual person. There is currently no place for spirituality within science, politics, business, or academia. To a five-sensory personality that lacks reverence, a reverent businessman or businesswoman appears to be competing at a disadvantage, because the range of his or her activities is not unlimited, and a reverent politician appears to be unqualified for leadership in a world where the only power that is recognized is external power. Yet, to the multisensory human, a reverent businessman or businesswoman is a person who infuses a new energy into the archetype of entrepreneur, shifting it from a dynamic that is motivated by profits that are generated by serving others to a dynamic of serving others that is made possible by profits, and a reverent politician is a person who challenges the concept of external power, and brings to the political arena the concerns of the heart. Therefore, the decision to approach Life with reverence means acting and thinking as a spiritual person in a world that does not recognize spirit, and it means moving consciously toward the perceptions of the multisensory human.

To live with reverence means being willing to say, "That is Life, we must not harm it," and "Those are our fellow humans, we must not destroy them," and mean it. It means reexamining the way that we treat the members of the animal kingdom that serve us so patiently. It means recognizing the rights of the Earth. That the Earth has rights is a concept that is not even present in our species yet.

An attitude of reverence is the atmosphere, the environment, in which the multisensory personality evolves. It is a sense of richness and fullness and intimacy of being. It creates compassion and acts of kindness. Without reverence, without the perception of the holiness of all things, the world becomes cold and barren, mechanical and random at the same time, and this creates experiences of alienation and acts of violence. It is not natural for us to live without reverence, because that separates us from the basic energy of the soul.

Reverence automatically brings forth patience. Impatience is the desire to have your needs met first. When your needs are taken care of, do you not then have patience with the needs of others? A reverent person honors Life in all its forms and all its activities. It does not think in the terms that are required to produce impatience.

Reverence permits non-judgmental justice. The soul does not judge, and so the personality chooses to bring into physical reality another of its soul's characteristics when it chooses to approach Life with reverence. The reverent person cannot consider himself or herself superior to another person or to any other form of Life, because the reverent person sees Divinity in all forms of Life, and honors it.

An attitude of reverence facilitates the transition from the logic and understanding of the five-sensory human to the higher order of logic and understanding of the multisensory human, because, as we shall see, this higher order of logic and understanding originates in the heart.

Without reverence, our experiences are brutal and destructive. With reverence, our experiences become compassionate and caring. We shall come to honor all of Life sooner or later. Our choices are when that shall happen, and the quality of experience that we shall have as we learn.*

---

* To learn how to apply what you have learned in this chapter and deepen your experiences, see the Chapter 3 Study Guide on page 256.

4

Heart

The logics that have served our five-sensory exploration of physical reality cannot comprehend evolution without time or the influence of the present upon the past. They cannot meaningfully represent the existence of the soul or a dynamic of energy balancing that generates and links many lifetimes. They reflect no experiential points of reference beyond those of the five-sensory personality. Therefore, the time has come for a higher order of logic and understanding.

The logics and understandings of the five-sensory personality originate in the mind. They are products of the intellect. The higher order of logic and understanding that is capable of meaningfully reflecting the soul comes from the heart. The creation of this higher order of logic and understanding, therefore, requires close attention to feelings.

The central position of the heart in the higher order of logic and understanding of the multisensory human, and the sensitivity to emotional currents that is characteristic of multisensory humans, appear as extraneous to the five-sensory personality because they do not serve the accumulation of external power. As we have come to seek and wield external power consciously, we have come to view feelings as unnecessary appendages, like tonsils—useless, but capable of creating pain and dysfunction. Thus, the pursuit of external power has led to a repression of emotion. This is true of us as individuals and as a species.

The irrelevancy that we attribute to feelings pervades our thinking and our values. We admire the "hard-nosed" businessman who fires employees for the sake of external power. We reward the military officer who sends himself or others to pain and death for the sake of external power. We honor the statesman who is not swayed by compassion.

When we close the door to our feelings, we close the door to the vital currents that energize and activate our thoughts and actions. We cannot begin the process of understanding the effects of our emotions upon us, our environment, and other people, or the effects of the emotions of other people upon themselves, their environment, and us. Without an awareness of our emotions, we cannot associate the effects of anger, sadness, grief, and joy—within ourselves or others—with their causes. We cannot distinguish between that part of us which is personality and that part of us which is soul. Without an awareness of our feelings we cannot experience compassion. How can we share the sufferings and the joys of others if we cannot experience our own?

If we are not intimate with our emotions, we cannot perceive the dynamics that lie behind emotions, the way that these dynamics work, and the ends that they serve. Emotions are currents of energy that pass through us. Awareness of these currents is the first step in learning how our experiences come into being and why.

Emotions reflect intentions. Therefore, awareness of emotions leads to awareness of intentions. Every discrepancy between a conscious intention and the emotions that accompany it points directly to a splintered aspect of the self that requires healing. If, for example, your intention to marry causes pain instead of joy, following the pain will lead you to unconscious intentions. If your intention to advance in your work causes sorrow instead of satisfaction, following the sorrow will lead you to unconscious intentions.

Without an awareness of your emotions you are not able to experience reverence. Reverence is not an emotion. It is a way of being, but the path to reverence is through your heart, and only an awareness of your feelings can open your heart.

The higher order of logic and understanding of the multisensory personality reveals connections where no connections are apparent to the five-sensory personality, and meaning where no meaning is apparent to the five-sensory personality. A five-sensory personality is not able to process fully the data of its senses. Its perception of reality is segmented. Its experience of the Universe is partitioned.

The five-sensory personality can learn that internal dynamics affect perception, and formulate this as folklore or cliché, such as, "Smile and the world smiles with you." It can discover regularities within physical reality, and formulate them as laws, such as, "A body in uniform motion will remain in uniform motion until it is acted upon by a force." Yet, the five-sensory personality is not able to experience the relationships between these domains, and, therefore, is not able to learn about one from the other. It is not able to experience the same richness through each.

Science, for example, reflects the Divine impulse to become conscious of relationships that connect apparently separate aspects of experience. It is the pinnacle achievement of the five-sensory personality, yet when the fruits of science are grasped only with the logic and understanding of the five-sensory human, internal dynamics—feelings and intentions—appear to be unrelated to the world of matter. Neither supernovas nor subatomic decay rates nor anything in between appear to be affected by what human beings feel or think.

When the discoveries of science are comprehended with the logic and understanding of the multisensory human, intimate relationships appear between internal dynamics and regularities that govern physical phenomena. To the multisensory human, for example, "A body in uniform motion will remain in uniform motion until it is acted upon by a force," reflects not only a dynamic at work within the realm of time and space and matter, but also a deeper dynamic that works within nonphysical reality as well.

How is this?

One of my friends in infantry officer candidate school was a tall, affable, and pleasant-looking young man from Kentucky named Hank. Hank and I liked each other early on. Several times he lent me his physical strength when my load became too heavy, and I helped him through intellectual obstacles, such as calculating artillery trajectories. We shared adventures, and our friendship grew.

Upon graduation, we were assigned to different organizations. I lost track of Hank until I ran into him in Saigon. He had been wounded, and due to the befriending of an Army General, had been assigned to a unit that I came frequently to visit. While serving in Saigon he met a popular female radio announcer, and they became engaged. It seemed a perfect match—a tall, handsome captain and a beautiful and admired public figure.

I again lost track of Hank until I had left the army. He called me to say that his wife was coming to make an appearance at a resort near me, and he asked me to meet him there. When I met Hank, now a civilian also, he looked troubled, and his easygoing manner was dampened. He had changed his name to Hal, he told me, and apologized that his wife was unable to join us. We spoke for a while, and when I asked him what he was doing with himself, he told me, "Looking for my place in the sun."

The next news that I heard of Hank/Hal was that he had killed himself. When I was later able to meet his widow, she told me a painful story of marital difficulties, of Hank's despondency, and of his suicide. In the years immediately following the Vietnam war, the rate of suicides among Vietnam veterans was significantly higher than the rate of suicides among nonveterans. Therefore, it is likely that Hank, also, was affected adversely by his experiences in Vietnam. Yet there was also a more common dynamic at work in my friend.

Hank was not the kind of person to ask himself deeper questions about his life. He did not inquire into the deeper meaning of his existence upon the Earth, because that would have caused him to change his life, and he did not want to do that. He lived his life without much reflection, and one day he awoke to overwhelming emptiness and powerlessness.

How does my friend's life relate to the first law of motion, "A body in uniform motion will remain in uniform motion until it is acted upon by a force"? What does "uniform motion" mean in terms of a human life, and what is the "force" that alters that motion?

The outward events of Hank's life were not uniform. He grew up on a farm in Kentucky, became a military officer, traveled thousands of miles from his home, married a celebrity, and brought his own life to an end. It was the unconscious quality of the flow of Hank's life that was uniform in its motion. Neither the experiences of his childhood nor his military service nor his marriage caused Hank to consider seriously the deeper meaning of his existence. The pains and the joys that flowed through him did not affect his awareness of who he was, or what he might become.

Hank did not allow himself to follow the experiences of his life to their roots. On the contrary, he feared such a pursuit. As a result, his life flowed uniformly unaware, uniformly unconscious, from its incarnation to its release. He experienced the situations that were necessary to the balancing of the energy of his soul, he responded to them in accordance with the conditioning that he had acquired through the karma of his soul and the environment into which he was born, and he created more karma unconsciously with each response.

The compassion that Hank brought into the world nurtured many people around him, including me, but he did not allow it to become his center of gravity. Hank made no effort to move toward his soul. He spent his life attempting to fulfill the wants of his personality, and he became too attached to those wants to attempt to change them. Thus, Hank's life was a "body in uniform motion" that never encountered a "force."

What is the "force" that Hank's life did not encounter?

Gregory was a white, middle-class, college-educated man from the Northeast. His childhood was emotionally difficult, and he grew up angry, manipulative, and bitter. He was incapable of forming relationships, and his violent temper and argumentative nature kept people at a distance. This further increased Gregory's disdain for Life and for other people, but he did not stop to ask what role he played in his experiences.

When, at last, his temper and his disagreeable disposition

caused the woman that he was living with to leave, Gregory fell into a deep anguish not only because of his loss, but also because he recognized in this latest event the repetition of a long-standing pattern in which he found himself, in each instance, suffering from rejection. He determined to confront both his pain and his pattern. He made arrangements to live in solitude while he searched within himself for the deepest causes of his painful life.

When he emerged, weeks later, both his perceptions and his values had changed. He began to soften, and, slowly, his old mannerisms dropped away. Over the following years he developed a more sensitive way of being with people. His cynicism gave way to an emerging joy, his anger melted, and other people became central to his life. He is a productive person now, and he draws his strength from the contributions that he makes to his fellows.

These changes did not come easily to Gregory. His transition from an angry, manipulative, disdainful person to a more caring and considerate person was a journey through pain that required much courage. Yet, by committing himself to that journey, he changed his life. From the point of view of Gregory's consciousness, the uniform flow of Gregory's life was altered significantly by his determination to confront his pain, and was altered further by his determination to cultivate his new perceptions. The "force" that altered the "uniform motion" of Gregory's life was his decision to enter into his life consciously. Without this decision, Gregory's life would have continued, as did Hank's, on the unconscious course that his karma, and his responses to the situations that it generated, would have created for him.

Is it appropriate to interpret the first law of motion—which depicts the idealized movement of a physical object—in this way? Is the first law of motion, when it is interpreted in this way, merely a metaphor that conveniently serves to describe a nonphysical dynamic? It is more than that. It is the reflection in physical reality—in the world of physical objects and phenomena—of a larger nonphysical dynamic at work in nonphysical domains. This is the physics of the soul. When science and its discoveries are understood with the higher order of logic and understanding of the multisensory human, they reveal the same richness that Life, itself, displays everywhere and endlessly.

The perception of the multisensory personality is not segmented. The multisensory human, for example, sees that the paradigms which form the history of science also reveal a history of the way that our species has seen itself in relation to the Universe: Ptolemaic astronomy reflects a species that sees itself as the center of the Universe; Copernican astronomy reflects a more sophisticated and interdependent perspective of a species that recognizes itself as part of the motion of the Universe; Newtonian physics reflects a species that is confident in its ability to grasp the dynamics of the physical world through the intellect; relativity reflects a species that understands the limiting relationship between the absolute and personalized perceptions of it; and quantum physics reflects a species that is becoming aware of the relationship of its consciousness to the physical world.

In other words, from the point of view of the multisensory human, the discoveries of science illuminate both inner and outer experiences, physical and nonphysical dynamics. A foundational discovery of optics, for example, is that white and black are not colors, like blue, green, and red. White is a combination of all the colors of the visible spectrum of light, and black is the absence of that spectrum. In other words, white is an integration of all the visible forms of radiance, and black is an absence of radiance.

What nonphysical dynamics does this discovery illuminate?

In European literature, white is associated with purity, goodness, and rightness. It is the symbol of positive and protective energy. Heroes and heroines dress in white. God's messengers and Heaven are associated with white. Angels are painted in robes of white. Black is associated with evil. Villains wear black. Black is the symbol of destruction. The day that catastrophe strikes is called a black day. Black represents despair, anger, and rage, which are absences of love, compassion, and forgiveness. A person who feels these things is said to be in a black mood.

"Dark Ages" are said to be a time when the "light of reason" was absent. The suffering of a splintered psyche, a psyche without radiance, is called the "dark night of the soul." The Devil is called the Prince of Darkness, and Hell is said to be a place where the Light of God does not reach.

Is the perception of white as an integration, or a completion, and black as an absence, therefore, limited in accuracy or applicability to the physical phenomena of white light and blackness? No. Language, mythology, religion, and science of the West each recognize in white a reflection of integration, or wholeness, or completion, and in black a reflection of the absence of this. The multisensory personality sees directly that each of these ways of understanding reflects the same thing.

The five-sensory personality cannot see in this way, and, therefore, its logics and understandings are not as comprehensive. The nature of wholeness and the lack of it, and the effects of each, are not discernible through the study of physical phenomena to a personality that is not able to see that both physical phenomena and the relationships between them are simultaneously parts of and reflections of larger patterns of life.

A personality that is not whole lives in a state of splinteredness, as represented by individual colors, or combinations of them. A personality that is not splintered lives in a state of wholeness, as represented by white light. A personality that loses touch with its soul, that loses the source of its Light, is a personality that has become capable of what we call evil, as represented by blackness.

What we call evil is the absence of Light, of love, in all cases. When we speak poetically of Light we associate it with purity, insight, and Divine inspiration. As we shall see, this type of Light is not merely poetical. It is real.

A soul can find it difficult to walk the way of Light through the course of an incarnation. It can find that learning to live in Light is a difficult sojourn. Through the choices that it makes while it is incarnate upon the Earth—the choice of anger instead of forgiveness, for example, or condemnation instead of understanding—a soul accumulates negative karma. As it leaves its body, it remains enveloped with the quality of Light that it acquired through the choices that it made while it was upon the Earth. When that soul has to create another personality, it will have to create a personality that is drawn from this well. Therefore, it will create a personality of more limitations.

A personality with limitations of consciousness will find what we call evil more attractive than will one with a more expanded awareness. The temptation to walk that way will be strong for such a personality. All souls are tempted, but an individual with limitations of consciousness will find it more attractive to walk into the magnetic field of fear because it would not recognize fear for what it is. It would accept it as something else, as something that is normal to Life.

How we understand evil, therefore, is very significant. Evil needs to be understood for what it is: the dynamic of the absence of Light. It is not something that one should prepare to battle, to run from, or to outlaw. Understanding evil as the absence of Light automatically requires that we reach for this thing called Light.

Conscious Light is equal to Divinity, to Divine Intelligence. Where there is an absence of Divine Intelligence, that darkness itself maneuvers. It is simply that there is darkness, and we stumble in the darkness. The existence in darkness is not permanent. Every soul will eventually be fully en-Lightened. A soul with no Light will always come to know Light because there is so much assistance provided to each soul at all times. There is much Light, as we shall see, that is continually surrounding such a soul even though it may not be able to directly penetrate it, and there is much assistance for souls that insist upon living in darkness. The encouragement to take even one thought into Light is always available. Eventually, they always do.

Understanding that evil is the absence of Light does not mean that it is inappropriate to respond to evil.

What is the appropriate response to evil?

The remedy for an absence is a presence. Evil is an absence and, therefore, it cannot be healed with an absence. By hating evil, or one who is engaged in evil, you contribute to the absence of Light and not to its presence. Hatred of evil does not diminish evil, it increases it.

The absence of Light causes the personality to suffer. There is pain. When you hate, you bring that suffering upon yourself. Hatred of evil affects the one who hates. It makes him or her a hateful person, a person who also has absented himself or herself from Light.

Understanding evil as the absence of Light does not require you to become passive, or to disregard evil actions or evil behavior. If you see a child being abused, or a people being oppressed, for example, it is appropriate that you do what you can to protect the child, or to aid the people, but if there is not compassion in your heart also for those who abuse and oppress—for those who have no compassion—do you not become like them? Compassion is being moved to and by acts of the heart, to and by the energy of love. If you strike without compassion against the darkness, you yourself enter the darkness.

Understanding that evil is the absence of Light challenges the perception of power as external. Can an absence be defeated? An evil person can be arrested, but can evil be arrested? An evil group can be imprisoned, but can evil be imprisoned? A compassionate heart is more effective against evil than an army. An army can engage another army, but it cannot engage evil. A compassionate heart can engage evil directly—it can bring Light where there was no Light.

Understanding evil as the absence of Light requires you to examine the choices that you make each moment in terms of whether they move you toward Light or away from it. It allows you to look with compassion upon those who engage in evil activities, even as you challenge their activities, and thus protects you from the creation of negative karma. It permits you to see that the place to begin the task of eliminating evil is within yourself. This is the appropriate response to evil.

The higher order of logic and understanding that characterizes the multisensory human permits it to learn more quickly than the five-sensory human is able to learn from what its senses alone tell it, and what its intellect makes of that. We have evolved as far as the intellect will take us. We have explored the scope and depth of five-sensory reality, and we have discovered the limitations of external power.

The next phase of our evolution will take us into the experiences of the multisensory human and the nature of authentic power.

This requires the heart.*

---

* To learn how to apply what you have learned in this chapter and deepen your experiences, see the Chapter 4 Study Guide on page 262.

CREATION

5

Intuition

The central perception of the multisensory human is that he or she is not alone. The multisensory human does not need to rely solely upon his or her own perceptions and interpretations of events for guidance, because he or she is in conscious communication with other, more advanced intelligences. This does not mean that the multisensory human is relieved thereby from choosing, in each instant, the course of his or her life, but it does mean that the multisensory human has conscious access to compassionate and impersonal help in the analysis of his or her possible choices, their probable consequences, and in the exploration of the different parts of himself or herself.

The five-sensory human is not alone either, but the five-sensory human is not aware of the assistance that is continually being given to him or her, and, therefore, cannot draw upon that assistance consciously. The five-sensory human must learn primarily through his or her physical experiences, and this learning takes longer because lessons that are learned in this way must come through the density of physical matter. A person that needs to learn the lesson of trust, for example, will experience a distrust of others. This distrust will create misunderstandings, and these will lead to tensions and unpleasant experiences. A five-sensory human will continue to experience the unpleasantnesses that result from his or her distrust of others until, in this lifetime or another, he or she realizes through interactions with others the source of these unpleasantnesses and takes steps to change it.

If a person is not able to trust, for example, he or she will interpret erroneously the words and actions of others. If a wife tells her husband that she must attend a business meeting, although she would like to be with him, and if her husband is unable to trust, he may take her meaning as a rejection, or as a signal that her work is more important to her than he is. This misunderstanding results from his inability to accept what his wife has told him, from his inability to trust her. As the wife continually experiences her husband's misunderstandings, they generate within her feelings of surprise, sorrow, frustration, anger, resentment, and, eventually, the rejection that her husband mistakenly perceived. Thus the husband, through the dynamic of distrust, creates his most significant fear.

The loss of a mate, or a friend, or a colleague through distrust is not a punishment for distrustfulness. It is the result of refusing to look consciously within oneself at the issue of trust. It is an experience that results from choosing repeatedly to distrust instead of to trust. A distrustful person will create unpleasant or painful situations until, at last, they bring him or her to the issue of trust. This may take five painful experiences, or five lifetimes of painful experiences, or fifty, but, eventually, this path will lead to and through the great lesson of trust.

The same dynamic applies to every personality characteristic that is not an expression of compassion and harmony. An angry personality, for example, will create unpleasant, or even tragic situations, until its anger is faced and removed as a block to its compassion and love, to the energy of its soul. The same is true for greedy personalities, selfish personalities, manipulating personalities, and so forth. This is the way that we have evolved until now.

A multisensory human can learn more rapidly than a five-sensory human. With the help that is available to it, the multisensory personality can understand more quickly the meaning of its experiences, how they come into being, what they represent, and its role in creating them. It does not need to experience twelve or twenty or two hundred painful experiences to learn a major lesson of trust, or responsibility, or humbleness. This does not necessarily mean that multisensory personalities do not experience painful situations, but that they have the capability of learning more quickly from them than five-sensory personalities, and, therefore, are more quickly able to choose more wisely, and with more compassion.

It is not necessary to be capable of voice-to-voice communication, so to speak, to be able to draw upon the sources of guidance and assistance that surround you. This way is available to the advanced multisensory human, but the road to that ability is a joyful one of developing an awareness that wise and compassionate guidance is always available to you, and learning to incorporate it consciously into your life.

How does this happen?

The five-sensory personality accepts every impulse and insight as his or her own, as originating within his or her psyche. The multisensory personality knows that this is not always the case. Impulses, hunches, sudden insights, and subtle insights have assisted us on our evolutionary path since the origin of our species. That we have not recognized the guidance that has come to us in this way is a consequence of seeing reality through only five senses. From the five-sensory point of view, there is no other place from which insights and hunches can come.

From the multisensory point of view, insights, intuitions, hunches, and inspirations are messages from the soul, or from advanced intelligences that assist the soul on its evolutionary journey. The multisensory personality, therefore, honors intuition in a way that the five-sensory personality does not. To the five-sensory personality, intuitions are curiosities. To the multisensory personality, they are promptings from, and links to, a perspective of greater comprehension and compassion than its own.

To the five-sensory personality, intuitive insights, or hunches, occur unpredictably, and cannot be counted upon. To the multisensory personality, intuitive insights are registrations within its consciousness of a loving guidance that is continually assisting and supporting its growth. Therefore, the multisensory personality strives to increase its awareness of this guidance.

The first step to this is becoming aware of what you are feeling. Following your feelings will lead you to their source. Only through emotions can you encounter the force field of your own soul. That is the human passage in a word.

The husband who was not able to trust, for example, may have felt anger, or shame, or resentment, or coldness toward his wife when she told him of her business appointment. If he had been able to experience his feelings consciously, to detach from them, to observe them as energy currents running through his system, he would have been able to ask himself, "Why does the news of this business meeting affect me in this way?" This would have allowed him to discover that his feelings were reflecting a sense of rejection, or of being less important to his wife than her meeting.

If he then had reviewed his wife's message, he would have seen that she had told him that she would have preferred to be with him, but could not. This would have allowed him to ask, "Then why do I still feel so disturbed?" and this would have led him to the answer, "Because I do not trust that she actually would prefer to be with me." In this way, becoming aware of his feelings, rather than unconsciously acting them out, would have led him to his issue of trust.

Having unearthed so much, he then could have asked himself, "Does my experience with my wife support this suspicion that she is not being honest with me?" If the answer to this question had been, "No, my experience is that she is a person of integrity," the husband could have come to see that the dynamic in motion within him did not relate to his wife, although her words triggered it. It would have allowed him to see the actual intention of his wife, and his feelings toward her would have softened. Her response to him would have been one of closeness toward a loving husband, instead of hurt caused by the rejection of her intimacy by a hostile husband.

Had he followed this course, he would not have had to ruin his afternoon, or his marriage. He would have been able to learn from his emotions, and his questions about them, the same lesson that he eventually would learn through the unpleasant experiences that resulted from his lack of trust. He would have been able to see within the framework of one instance the effects of distrust, and the effects of trust.

Each question that a person asks, such as, "Why does news of this business meeting affect me this way?", "Why do I feel so disturbed?", and "Does my experience support my suspicion?", invokes guidance. Every time you ask for guidance, you receive it. Every time you ask yourself, "What is my motivation?", you ask the Universe, "Help me to see," and help comes. You may not always be capable of hearing the answers to your questions when you ask them, and the answers may not always come in the ways that you expect, but they always come. Sometimes an answer occurs in the form of a feeling—a yes feeling or a no feeling—sometimes in the form of a memory, or a thought that, at the time, seems random, sometimes in a dream and sometimes in the form of a realization that is prompted by an experience that will occur the next day.

No question is unheard, and no question goes un-answered. "Ask and you shall receive" is the rule, but you must learn how to ask and how to receive.

The intellect is meant to expand perceptions, to help you grow in perceptual strength and complexity, and not to do harm. The experiences of the intellect are experiences of knowledge. Knowledge is power, and for each level of knowledge, you are held responsible for how you use it. Knowledge that simply comes into your being and does not in some way or form become processed and used to the benefit of others can have a seriously detrimental effect upon your body. Karmic obligations that are created by deliberate misuse of knowledge, by knowingly harming or creating discord in another, are greater than those that are created in ignorance.

In a world that understands power as external, the intellect often functions without the compassionate influence of the heart. This creates situations in which intellectual power is used as a weapon to harm others, to exert willpower without tenderness. When the intellect is used to design or develop or produce weapons, for example, it is not being used as it was intended. When an industry, or a plant, is designed or built or operated without consideration for its effects upon the Earth, upon human life, and upon the environment, the intellect is not being used as it was intended. When you plan to profit at another's expense, you are not using your intellect as it was intended.

In a world of five-sensory humans that understand power as external, intuitive knowledge is not regarded as knowledge, and, therefore, it is not processed. It is not submitted to the intellect. It is not expanded or studied or made technical and disciplined. Just as we were taught to develop and employ cognition—to think things through—so, too, can we learn to develop and employ intuition—to ask for guidance and receive it. Just as there are technologies to discipline the mind, such as analytical thinking, studying, repetition, and respect for the mechanism, so, too, are there techniques to engage and discipline the intuition.

The first of these is to honor emotional cleansing at all times. If you are emotionally blocked and you cannot, or you do not, know what you feel, or if you have blocked what you feel so effectively that you become emotionless, you become a negative person, and you also create a physically diseased body. By keeping your emotions clear, emotional negativity does not reside in you, and you become lighter and lighter. This opens your intuitive track because it allows you a clear sense of loving. It brings you closer to unconditional love and renders you harmless. It lightens the quality of your frequency, so to speak, and therefore the guidance that you receive is clear and unobstructed as it enters your system.

This requires that you clear yourself each day of your emotional impacts. Just as you dispose of your physical body wastes and toxins, so, too, dispose of your emotional wastes and toxins by finishing emotionally unfinished business, by not going to bed in anger, by seeing that you do not feel contaminated emotionally, and by learning to work with and to honor your emotional currents of energy.

The second is a cleansing nutritional program. Being physically toxic interferes with intuition.

The third is to honor the guidance that you receive. Emotional and physical cleansing leads to intuition, and this leads to learning to respond. You must be willing to hear what your intuition says and act accordingly. Many people do not wish to hear what can be heard so easily, and, therefore, they deny that they hear anything.

The fourth is to allow yourself an orientation of openness toward your life and the Universe, to approach the questions in your life with a sense of faith and trust that there is a reason for all that is happening, and that that reason, at its heart, is always compassionate and good. This is an essential thought that needs to be in place in order to activate and cultivate intuition.

What is intuition, and how does it work?

Intuition is perception beyond the physical senses that is

meant to assist you. It is that sensory system which operates without data from the five senses. Your intuitional system is a part of your incarnation. When you leave your body, you will leave behind the intuitional system that was developed for you, as you will leave behind your personality, because it will no longer be necessary.

Intuition serves many purposes. Intuition serves survival. It prompts you to pursue that which has no apparent reason in order to survive. Hunches about danger, for example, about what is risky and what is not, about which street is safe to walk and which is not, or about checking the car under the hood, help you to remain in the physical world.

Intuition serves creativity. It tells you what book to buy for your project. It tells you where to meet the colleague that you need to meet, and which ideas from one field will complement which ideas from another. It is the hunch that a certain painting should be done in gray, and that another should be done in purple. It is the sense that an idea that has never been tried before might work.

Intuition serves inspiration. It is the sudden answer to a question. It is the meaning that takes form in the fog of confusion. It is the Light that comes to the darkness. It is the presence of the Divine.

Intuition can be thought of as a type of wiring that can be used by various sources. One of these sources is the soul. Intuition is a walkie-talkie, so to speak, between the personality and the soul. This happens through the higher self.

The higher self is the connecting link when the soul

speaks to its personality. It is the dialogue between the personality and its immortal self. The personality-soul communication is the higher self experience, but the personality does not communicate with the fullness of its soul.

All of the energy of the soul does not incarnate. To incarnate, the soul creates a personality from those parts of itself that it wants to heal in the physical environment, and from those parts of itself that it lends to the process of healing in that lifetime.

So powerful is the energy of the soul that it could not advance into a physical form without, literally, exploding that form. In the creation of a personality, the soul calibrates parts of itself, reduces parts of itself, to take on the human experience. Your higher self is that aspect of your soul that is in you, but it is not the fullness of your soul. It is a smaller soul self. Therefore, "higher self" is another term for "soul," yet the soul is more than the higher self.

Picture a cup, a gallon, and a water tank. The water tank is the soul. An aspect of the soul becomes a gallon. That gallon is still soul, but not the fullness of the soul. It is that part of the soul that is on mission, so to speak. The personality is the cup. The cup contacts the gallon, the higher self soul, but not the full-bodied water tank.

Communication between the personality and its soul is an in-house intuitive process. It is a process that is organic to your own internal system. For example, decision making, which is your process, can be an intuitive process in which you pull data from your mind, your heart, and your intuition, relying upon the guidance of your higher self. Each of these sources is part of your own system of energy. Your personality and your higher self are of your soul.

Intuition also can permit the personality, through its higher self, to receive information from other souls of higher process, souls that are not its own soul. Sources of guidance other than your own higher self can come across on the same radio station, so to speak. This is not the same as an intuitive process. This is a process of receiving guidance through intuitive channels.

Receiving information through intuitive channels is significantly different from receiving information through intutive processes. Receiving information through intuitive processes is cooking at home. Receiving information through intuitive channels is ordering out.

The guidance that the multisensory human receives through intuitive processes and through intuitive channels is as essential for his or her well-being and growth as sunshine and clean air. Through his or her intuition, the multisensory human comes to understand and to experience truth consciously.

What is truth?

Truth is that which does not contaminate you, but empowers you. Therefore, there are degrees of truth, but, generically, truth is that which can do no harm. It cannot harm.

Higher self connecting to nonphysical teachers produces a level of truth that is true not just for you, but that would be true for anyone who came into contact with it. If you subtracted everything that is personal to you from the guidance that you receive through intuitive channels, there would remain a kernel of truth that would apply to others, or, at least, the presence of unconditional love, whereas much of the information that you receive through your own intuitive process will be effective only for you. This is the difference between personal truth and impersonal truth. They are both truth, but personal truth is yours, and impersonal truth belongs to all that is, to each person. We need truth to grow in the same way that we need vitamins, affection, and love.

At times, the truth that comes through intuitive processes or through intuitive channels can be contaminated with your own fear. Here is a place to apply your intellect. In other words, you might think that you are receiving a clear intuition, but if you examine it rationally, if you take it apart, you will be able to see that you are responding to an insecurity, just as the question "Does my experience with my wife support my suspicion?" would have allowed the husband to see that the origin of his emotional response was an insecurity rather than the energy dynamic with his wife. Answers that come through your intuitive processes or through intuitive channels may challenge what you would prefer to do. Your lower self, your personality, will not challenge, but rationalize.

It is natural to ascend to a level where you can learn to distinguish between the sources of guidance that you receive. The idea of being guided by truth that is received intuitively appears unusual to the five-sensory personality. The psychology that has been constructed upon the experiences of the five-sensory personality does not even recognize intuition in the sense that it recognizes, and studies and seeks to understand, physical perception, affect, and cognition. To the multisensory personality, it is unusual *not* to rely upon truths that it receives from its higher self and, through its higher self, from souls that are more advanced.

The personality is never separate from its soul, and the soul and its personalities are continually assisted and guided with impersonal compassion and wisdom. This is so for both the five-sensory personality and for the multisensory personality, but the five-sensory personality is not aware of its soul or the guidance that it receives from its higher self and from more advanced souls. The multisensory personality is aware of its soul—it seeks to align itself with its soul, to become the physical embodiment of its higher self—and it consciously invokes and receives the loving assistance of its own soul and of other souls that assist it.*

---

* To learn how to apply what you have learned in this chapter and deepen your experiences, see the Chapter 5 Study Guide on page 267.

— 6 —

Light

The soul is not physical, yet it is the force field of your being. The higher self is not physical, yet it is the living template of the evolved human, the fully awakened personality. The experience of intuition cannot be explained in terms of the five senses, because it is the voice of the nonphysical world. Therefore, it is not possible to understand your soul or your higher self or your intuition without coming to terms with the existence of nonphysical reality.

Knowing in the cognitive sense cannot produce proof of nonphysical reality any more that it can produce proof of God. Proof of nonphysical reality does not exist in the dimension that the rational mind seeks it. Therefore, when you ask from the perspective of the five-sensory personality,

"Does nonphysical reality exist?" what you really are asking is, "If I cannot prove the existence of nonphysical reality, do I decide that it is nonsensical? Do I decide that there is no answer, or do I expand myself to the level at which the answer can be given?"

When a mind asks a question that suggests a different level of truth, no matter what the question, expansion has always been the way of the scientist, the pursuer of truth. At one time in our evolution, for example, the question was asked, "Are there forms of life that are smaller than the eye can see?" From the five-sensory perception, the answer was, "No." Someone did not accept that answer, and the microscope was invented. Then the question, "Do parts of nature exist that are smaller than what can be seen through a microscope?" was asked, and, again, from the five-sensory perception the answer was, "No," but we did not stop, and instead discovered, and developed a rich understanding of, atomic and subatomic phenomena.

As we created the tools to see, that which was once considered nonexistent became existent, but we had to expand first. The challenge, and the task, for the advanced or expanding mind is to expand to a level at which questions that cannot be answered from within the accepted understanding of truth can be answered.

What is nonphysical reality?

Nonphysical reality is your home. You came from nonphysical reality, you will return to nonphysical reality, and the larger part of you currently resides in, and evolves in, nonphysical reality. The same is true for each of the billions of human beings upon this planet. Therefore, the majority of your interactions with other human beings occurs in nonphysical reality. For example, when you think loving thoughts of someone who is close to you emotionally, such as a family member, you shift the quality of your consciousness, and this contributes to his or her energy system.

If a daughter who harbors resentment toward her father, for example, evolves into a deeper understanding of her relationship with him, such as an understanding of the karmic role that he has played in activating within her a major lesson of love or responsibility, and if her intention to heal herself and her relationship with her father is deep and clear, do not think, even for an instant, that her father is not aware of this, even if she does not speak to him. He is not aware consciously, but his whole being feels what she is doing. His conscious mind may feel it through sudden moments of sentimentalism about things that he had not thought about before, or he may suddenly look at pictures of his daughter as a young child and feel a pull in his heart even though he is not consciously aware of why he is feeling what he is feeling or doing what he is doing.

You participate in this form of data bank exchange, so to speak, with all the souls that you are close to, and, to some extent, with all the souls that touch your life. As you shift your data bank content and the information that you send to a soul, it is processed through his or her own system. It is at that level that the cause and effect of your intentions, the way that you choose to shape your energy, influences others.

How does this happen?

You are a system of Light, as are all beings. The frequency of your Light depends upon your consciousness. When you shift the level of your consciousness, you shift the frequency of your Light. If you choose to forgive someone who has wronged you, for example, rather than to hate that person, you shift the frequency of your Light. If you choose to feel affection, or kinship, with a person rather than distance or coldness, you shift the frequency of your Light.

Emotions are currents of energy with different frequencies. Emotions that we think of as negative, such as hatred, envy, disdain, and fear have a lower frequency, and less energy, than emotions that we think of as positive, such as affection, joy, love, and compassion. When you choose to replace a lower-frequency current of energy, such as anger, with a higher-frequency current, such as forgiveness, you raise the frequency of your Light. When you choose to allow higher-frequency currents of energy to run through your system, you experience more energy. When a person is despairing, for example, or anxious, he or she feels physically depleted because he or she has merged with an energy current of low frequency. A person in this situation becomes heavy and dull, whereas a joyous person abounds with energy, and feels buoyant, because he or she is running a higher-frequency current of energy through his or her system.

Different thoughts create different emotions. Thoughts of vengeance, violence, and greed, or thoughts of using others, for example, create emotions such as anger, hatred, jeal-

ousy, and fear. These are low-frequency currents of energy, and, therefore, they lower the frequency of your Light, or consciousness. Creative or loving or caring thoughts invoke high-frequency emotions, such as appreciation, forgiveness, and joy, and raise the frequency of your system. If your thoughts are thoughts that draw low-frequency energy currents to you, your physical and emotional attitudes will deteriorate, and emotional or physical disease will follow, whereas thoughts that draw high-frequency energy currents to you create physical and emotional health.

Lower-frequency systems pull energy from higher-frequency systems. If you are unaware of your emotions and your thoughts, your frequency will be lowered by—you will lose energy to—a system of lower frequency than your own. We say, for example, that a depressed person is "draining," or that he or she "sucks up energy." A system of sufficiently high frequency will soothe, or calm, or refresh you because of the effect of the quality of its Light upon your system. Such a system is "radiant."

By choosing your thoughts, and by selecting which emotional currents you will release and which you will reinforce, you determine the quality of your Light. You determine the effects that you will have upon others, and the nature of the experiences of your life.

"Light" represents consciousness. When we do not understand a thing, we say that we must "bring it to light." If we are confused, we say that our process "needs more light." When a sudden idea reorders our thoughts, we say that the "light came on," and when a person is fully conscious, we say that he or she is "enlightened." When you release a negative thought, or a negative feeling, you release lower-frequency currents of energy from your system, and this, literally, allows an increase in the frequency of your consciousness.

Thinking of the Universe in terms of light, frequencies, and energies of different frequencies—in the terms that have become familiar to us through the study of physical light—is not merely metaphorical. It is a natural and powerful way to think of the Universe because physical light is a reflection of nonphysical Light.

Physical light is not the Light of your soul. Physical light travels at a certain velocity. It cannot go faster. The Light of your soul is instantaneous. There is no time between a daughter's loving intention toward her father and the soul of her father understanding that intention. Instantaneousness, therefore, is very much a part of your life. In nonphysical reality, the decisions that you make in terms of how you choose to use your energy have effects that are instantaneous. They are one with who and what you are.

Energies that emanate from your soul have instantaneousness to them. Energies that emanate from your personality follow the path of physical light. Fear, for example, is an experience of the personality. The soul can be confused and away from Light, but it does not experience fear. If the soul experiences an absence of Light from a part of itself, the personality will experience this absence of Light as fear.

That fear is of the personality, and, therefore, of space and time. Unconditional love is of the soul, instantaneous, Universal, not bound.

Just as visible light is one portion, like an octave, in a continuum of energy of graduated frequencies that extends below and above what the eye can see, the continuum of nonphysical Light extends below and above, so to speak, the frequency range in which the human exists. The human experience is a particular frequency range in the continuum of nonphysical Light in the same way that visible light is a particular frequency range in the continuum of physical light.

Other intelligences inhabit other ranges of frequency. These forms of Life do not exist elsewhere from us. Just as infrared light, ultraviolet light, microwave light, and many, many other frequencies and ranges of frequencies coexist with the visible light spectrum, but are invisible to us, the Life forms that are characterized by different frequency ranges of nonphysical Light coexist with us, but are invisible to us. In the place that you now sit exist many different beings, or groups of beings, each active and evolving in its own reality and in its own way. These realities commingle with yours in the same way that microwave radiation exists alongside of visible light, but is undetectable to the human eye.

Our species is evolving from one frequency range in the spectrum of nonphysical Light into another, higher range of frequency. This is the evolution of the five-sensory personality into the multisensory personality. The multisensory personality is more radiant and energetic than the five-sensory personality. It is aware of the Light of its soul, and it is able to detect, and to communicate with, forms of Life that are invisible to the five-sensory personality.

The Universe is a hierarchy that has no bottom and no top. Between the levels of the hierarchy there is an understanding that higher perceptions can be a part of, and are encouraged to be a part of, the experience of lower plane spirits as they strive to expand their own awareness. Thus, there is always a higher level of assistance. You are involved in this process, although your personality is unaware of this, because it is done at the level of your soul.

There is much that the five-sensory personality is unaware of, and much that even a fully empowered multisensory personality will not remember until, at the end of its life, it returns to nonphysical reality. You are not aware of the many lifetimes of the past and future personalities of your soul, for example, but the intensity of parts of your being derives directly from these lifetimes, just as do some of your relationships. If an aspect of your being manifests physically, such as the aspect of you-as-teacher, or you-as-warrior, then there are connected nonphysical aspects that are also active and participating in the teaching, or the warring, dynamic from the nonphysical realms of which you are a part and bonded to. The aspect of self that you bring to bear in a physical moment represents a force that is many, many times more significant and complex.

Our nonphysical assistance comes from ranges of nonphysical Light that are higher in frequency than our own. The intelligences that assist and guide us, unconsciously in the case of the five-sensory personality, and consciously in the case of the multisensory personality, are of a higher rank in creation than we, and, therefore, can provide us with a quality of guidance and assistance that we cannot give to each other.

The five-sensory personality associates rank within a hierarchy with graduated levels of worth, and it associates a lower rank within a hierarchy with less worth, less ability to control others, and more vulnerability. From the point of view of the Universe, all the ranks of creation are of equal value, all are precious. When seen through authentically empowered eyes, a being with a higher rank in creation is one that has more ability to see without obstruction, more ability to live in love and wisdom, and more ability and desire to help others evolve into the same love and Light.

Each human soul has both guides and Teachers. A guide is not a Teacher. Guides are what might be thought of as experts in certain fields that are called in for consultation. If you are writing a book, for example, or creating a project, or organizing an event, a guide that has the quality of warmth, or creativity, or insight that you wish to incorporate into your work is available to you.

Teachers operate on a more personal plane of involvement, so to speak, although they are impersonal energies that we personalize, that we feel a personal relationship with. A nonphysical Teacher brings you ever closer to your soul. It draws your attention to the vertical path, and to the difference between the vertical path and the horizontal path.

The vertical path is the path of awareness. It is the path of consciousness and conscious choice. The person who chooses to advance his or her spiritual growth, to cultivate awareness of his or her higher self, is on a vertical path. The vertical path is the path of clarity. The potential for the creation of clarity and the experience of interacting with your nonphysical Teacher are one and the same.

The horizontal path is the path that satisfies your personality. A businessman or a businesswoman, for example, who devotes his or her life to the accumulation of money is on a horizontal path. No matter how diverse his or her ventures may become, they are essentially identical. If they make money, they please the personality, and if they lose money, they distress the personality, but they do not serve the higher self. They do not serve his or her spiritual growth.

A person that seeks relationships only to gratify his or her own needs, such as his or her own emotional or sexual needs, will find that each relationship is essentially identical, that the people in his or her life are replaceable, that experiences with the first and experiences with the second are essentially the same. This is the horizontal path. Each new experience is not really new. It is more of the same thing. To experience relationships of substance and depth requires approaching and entering into relationships with consciousness and concern for the other. That is the vertical path.

This does not mean that learning does not occur in all situations, and that when a horizontal path is no longer appropriate to a soul's learning, that soul will not leave it behind. Sooner or later, each soul will turn toward authentic power. Every situation serves this goal, and every soul will reach it. The vertical path begins with the decision to do that consciously.

Guides and Teachers assist the soul in every phase of its evolution. The number of guides and Teachers that a soul has depends upon what it seeks to accomplish and its level of awareness. Souls that take upon themselves projects of more magnitude bring to themselves more assistance.

Your soul knows its guides and Teachers. It drew upon their wisdom and compassion in charting the incarnation that became you, and that part of your soul that is you will be gathered into their waiting arms when the incarnation that is you comes to an end—when you go home. You receive loving guidance and assistance at each moment. At each moment, you are prompted and encouraged to move into Light.

The decisions that you make are yours to make. A nonphysical Teacher cannot, and would not, live your life for you. It will assist you through the learning experiences of your life. The answers that it can provide you depend upon the questions that you ask—by questioning your own motivations, by praying or meditating and remaining open for the answer, or by asking directly, as in the case of the multisensory human that has developed this ability. When you ask one set of questions, one set of doorways opens before you, and when you ask other questions, other doorways open.

In each instance, your Teacher, or Teachers, will advise

you with impersonal compassion and clarity. It will help you to examine the probable results of each choice that you make. It will touch your feelings in ways that bring your awareness to areas that need to be healed. It will answer your questions, but you must ask them, and, therefore, give direction to your own energy. It will advise you as to which courses will most likely lead to which results, and it will continue to advise you with wisdom and compassion no matter what choices you make.

A Teacher can neither create nor remove karma for you. No being, not even a nonphysical Teacher, can assume responsibility for your life, for the way that you choose to use your energy, but a nonphysical Teacher can help you to understand what your choices and your experiences represent. It can provide you with the knowledge that will allow you to choose responsibly, and hopefully, choose wisely. Therefore, the ability to draw consciously upon your nonphysical guidance and assistance, to communicate consciously with a nonphysical Teacher, is a treasure that cannot be described, a treasure beyond words and value.

Every decision that you make either moves you toward your personality, or toward your soul. Each decision that you make is an answer to the question "How do you choose to learn love?", "How do you choose to learn authentic empowerment—through doubt and fear, or through wisdom?" This is the heart of the Garden of Paradise story. The Tree of Truth, given unto the entire human species, said, "Learn! Which way do you wish to learn?"

This is the ultimate first act of free will: How do you wish to learn? The question continues in every one of your life situations. It is the eternal question. It is the longest-running show on Broadway, so to speak. No matter what situation, no matter what moment, the Garden of Eden question continues and continues and continues. Each time the opportunity in every circumstance in miniature is, "Will you choose the way of doubt and fear, or will you choose the Tree of Wisdom?"

The Tree of Life, of Knowledge, of Truth, of Wisdom, is an opportunity, an archetypical question. Adam and Eve, the male and female principles within the Garden of Eden, took the apple symbolically, and misused knowledge. Their choice was to misuse knowledge, and, therefore, they created shame. That was not part of the human design up to that point. The misuse of knowledge, of truth, of wisdom, produced embarrassment and shame. That gave rise to guilt. Guilt gave rise to fear, and so began the evolution of the human species.

The decision to take the apple was a decision of the highest order of evolution, an order that cannot be conceived, or even grappled with, in the same context that we would use to understand a human decision. To speak of decisions in terms of an individual human life, or in the terms of a larger body of individual human lives, is very different from speaking about how the role of evolution and learning began billions of years ago with the human species.

The decision to take the apple in the Garden of Eden

story does not refer to one decision that was made by two humans who really existed in such a setting. It was not a decision such as you or I would make in terms of, "Do I choose this or that?" The Garden of Paradise story describes the beginning of the whole experience of Earth and the human species. It refers to principles of energy that were brought to bear upon larger bodies of group consciousnesses that had stress, that had formation energies, creation energies. In their process of forming their own polarities, polarities that would become the polarities of the human experience, doubt and fear stood opposing to trust and Light, and so they came into being.

Yet, it is not inappropriate to understand the Garden of Eden story in terms of human choices between doubt and fear on the one hand and wisdom on the other, because the choice to learn through wisdom or through doubt and fear is very much part of every single challenge that every single human comes up against within every minute of every day, and this challenge reflects the dynamics that, at a larger level of evolution, were brought to bear upon our evolution.

This brings us to the relationship between choice, Light, and physical reality.*

---

* To learn how to apply what you have learned in this chapter and deepen your experiences, see the Chapter 6 Study Guide on page 273.

— 7 —

Intention I

Not all forms are physical. A thought, for example, is a form. What is a thought formed out of?

A thought is energy, or Light, that has been shaped by consciousness. No form exists without consciousness. There is Light, and there is the shaping of Light by consciousness. This is creation.

Energy continually pours through you, entering at the top of your head and descending downward through your body. You are not a static system. You are a dynamic being of Light that at each moment informs the energy that flows through you. You do this with each thought, with each intention.

The Light that flows through your system is Universal

energy. It is the Light of the Universe. You give that Light form. What you feel, what you think, how you behave, what you value, and how you live your life reflect the way that you are shaping the Light that is flowing through you. They are the thought forms, the feeling forms and the action forms that you have given to Light. They reflect the configuration of your personality, your space-time being.

You change the way that you shape the Light which is flowing through you by changing your consciousness. You do this, for example, when you challenge a negative pattern, such as anger, and consciously choose to replace it with compassion, or when you challenge impatience and consciously choose to understand and appreciate the needs of others. This creates different forms of thought, feeling, and action. It changes your experience.

Every experience, and every change in your experience, reflects an intention. An intention is not only a desire. It is the use of your will. If you do not like the relationship that you have with your husband or with your wife, for example, and you would like it to be different, that desire alone will not change your relationship. If you truly desire to change your relationship, that change begins with the intention to change it. How it will change depends upon the intention that you set.

If you intend that your relationship with your husband or your wife become harmonious and loving, that intention will open you to new perceptions. It will allow you to see the love that your husband or wife expresses for you in his or her own way, if that is the case. It will allow you to see the absence of that love, if that is the case. It will reorient you toward harmony and love so that you can see clearly from that perspective what is necessary to change your relationship, and if that is achievable.

If you intend to end your relationship, that ending begins with the intention to end. This intention will create in you a restlessness. You will feel less and less fulfilled with your mate. You will feel an openness to others in a way that you have not felt before. Your higher self has begun the search for another partner. When that partner appears, you will be drawn to him or to her, and, if you accept that partner, which also is an intention, a new path will open for you.

If you have conflicting intentions, you will be torn because both dynamics will be set in motion and oppose each other. If you are not aware of all of your intentions, the strongest one will win. You may have a conscious intention to improve your marriage, for example, and, simultaneously, an unconscious intention to end it. If the unconscious intention to end your marriage is stronger than the conscious intention to improve it, the dynamic of restlessness, lack of fulfillment, etc., eventually will overcome the conscious intention to become loving and harmonious within your marriage. In the end, your marriage will terminate.

If the conscious intention to transform your marriage is stronger than the unconscious intention to end it, and if your husband or your wife is essentially supportive, you will succeed, but the dynamic of opposing intentions within you will produce confusions and anguishes, perhaps for both of you, as you become open to new perceptions of love and harmony within your marriage, and, simultaneously, experience restlessness, lack of fulfillment, and openness to other partners.

This is the experience of a splintered personality. A splintered personality struggles with itself. The values, perceptions, and behaviors of a splintered personality are not integrated. A splintered personality is not conscious of all the parts of itself. A splintered personality is frightened. It fears aspects of itself that threaten what it seeks and what it has attained.

A splintered personality experiences the circumstances within its life as more powerful than itself. A splintered personality that has a conscious intention to improve its marriage, and a stronger, unconscious intention to end it, for example, will feel, after the collapse of its marriage, that despite its efforts, despite even its best efforts, things did not work out as it intended. This is not so. They worked out exactly as it intended, but, because she or he held conflicting intentions, much turbulence, so to speak, was created in the flow of the Light through that person.

If conflicting intentions are nearly balanced, and if a personality is not willing or able to acknowledge that an aspect, or aspects, of her self or his self stand opposed to her or his conscious intention, severe stress and emotional pain result. These can cause states of schizophrenia and physical illness. In less severe cases the anguish can be just as painful.

A splintered personality is a personality in need of healing. As a personality becomes conscious and integrated, it heals those parts of its soul that incarnated in order to be healed. The Light that flows through a whole personality is focused into a single, clear beam. Its intentions are powerful and effective. It becomes a laser, a phase-coherent beam of Light, a beam in which every wave precisely reinforces every other.

A whole personality is not like a laser. A laser is like a whole personality. Lasers are the reflection in physical reality of an energy dynamic that, until very recently, has not been central to the human experience. The development of the laser in the middle part of the twentieth century reflects within the physical arena a dynamic that is central to what our species is evolving into.

We are evolving into a species of whole individuals, individuals who are aware of their nature as beings of Light, and who shape their Light consciously, wisely, and with compassion. Therefore, the physical phenomenon of phase-coherent light, light that does not struggle with itself, so to speak, has come into being. It is a new phenomenon to the human experience, and it reflects the new energy dynamic of the whole human. The achievements of science, in other words, do not reflect the laboratory capabilities of individuals, or nations, but the spiritual capabilities of our species.

Intentions affect more than relationships. Intentions set into motion processes that affect every aspect of your life. If you desire to change your job, for example, that change begins with the intention to change. As the intention to leave your present job emerges into your consciousness, you begin to open yourself to the possibility of working somewhere else, or doing something else. You begin to feel less and less at home in what you are doing. Your higher self has begun the search for your next job.

When the opportunity appears, you are ready to accept it. You may require additional time to step into the new situation consciously, to make it your own, because it is human nature to resist change, but, if you accept it, your intention will manifest physically. It will assume a physical form.

Decisions such as where to work and whom to partner with and where to live are not the only type of decisions that you make, nor are they the decisions that have the most influence upon your life. At each instant you make decisions in the form of your attitudes about the Universe, about other people, and about yourself. You make these decisions continually and your experiences at each moment are created by them. You are a decision-making being.

A single choice to challenge your anger and replace it with understanding does not immediately change these attitudes, but it brings them, through your feelings, into awareness, and as you make the decisions of your life consciously and responsibly and wisely, your attitudes come to reflect your decisions. Eventually, the deepest decision-making processes within you—those that shape from moment to moment the Light that flows through you—become aligned with what you choose consciously, just as they are aligned, before you choose awareness, with what you choose unconsciously.

You create your reality with your intentions.

How does this happen?

Intentions shape Light. They set Light into motion. Each intention—anger, greed, jealousy, compassion, understanding—sets energy into motion, sets patterns of Light into motion. Physical matter is the densest, or heaviest, level of Light.

Physical reality is not a dead and empty stage on which Life evolves. Every physical form, as well as every nonphysical form, is Light that has been shaped by consciousness. No form exists apart from consciousness. There is not one planet in the Universe that does not have an active level of consciousness, although it may not be what we recognize as consciousness.

Physical reality and the organisms and the forms within physical reality are systems of Light within systems of Light, and this Light is the same Light as the Light of your soul. Each of these systems of Light is shaped by consciousness. The physical reality of the Earth school is shaped by the decisions of those who are in it.

What is the relationship between physical reality and the choices that you make in your life?

Reality is a multilayered creation. No two people have the same reality.

The first layer of your reality is your personal reality. This is your personal life, your personal sphere of influence.

Here your decisions are most effective, and are felt directly. By choosing to feel kindness instead of coldness, you change the frequency of your consciousness, and this changes your experiences. Within your personal reality, you can choose to be selfish or to be giving, to look upon yourself and others brutally or with compassion, to serve yourself or to serve others and the Earth. Each of these decisions shapes the Light that flows through you, and creates the reality within you. This reality spills over into the realities of those around you.

The second layer of your reality is your family. When individual human souls come together, they form a group energy field, a merger of soul energy in a group. Therefore, the decisions that you make within your personal reality, such as the decision to be giving or to be selfish, or the decision to be angry or to be understanding, contribute to the shaping of the reality that you share with your family. The same is true for each member of your family. Your father's dependability or drunkenness, for example, contributes to this level of your reality, as does your mother's timidness or assertiveness, and your sister's jealousy or support, etc. As you move into this layer of your reality, you move into an atmosphere that includes others within your life. While it is also personal, you are beginning to move outward from the intimacy of your personal reality.

The next layer of your reality is your school, or the place where you work. This level of reality is also a co-creation, and is more impersonal than the reality that you share with your family. Not all of the perceptions that are central to your personal reality are central to this reality. For example, you may have discovered that when you pray, you get answers, but this perception is not necessary to the functioning of your university, or your business. It may not be appropriate to share this perception with the person sitting beside you in the lecture hall, or with the receptionist in the front office.

The next layer of your reality includes those people that you come into contact with in the course of your living, such as the people from whom you buy your airline tickets, the people at the grocery store, and the bus drivers and the merchants in your town. The beliefs that you hold as a participant in this and other more impersonal layers of your reality also are not all as intimate and personal as the beliefs that you hold in your personal reality. In these arenas you share your personal beliefs that you feel are more aligned with the larger general atmosphere of beliefs upon our planet.

In other words, as you move outward from your personal reality, you move outward in bands of energy that are shared by more and more individuals with whom you have a great deal in common vibrationally. Most individuals, for example, understand "city," and "urban area." Most individuals understand "Europe," and "United States." These are shared collective perceptions, but they are not shared as widely as the perceptions of "water" and "air," which are universal perceptions upon our planet.

Not all the people on our planet know that there is a

place called "Europe." "Europe" is a majority perception upon our planet, but not a universal perception, such as "air." Consciously receiving answers to prayers is not a majority perception upon our planet. Therefore, you are free to tell the people at the grocery store that you hear answers when you pray, but you may decide not to share that perception for your own sense of safety, because you realize that their consciousnesses may not be able to accept that.

The next layer of your reality is your town or city, the next is your state, or area of the country, and the next is your culture, or nation. A nation is an aspect of the personality of Gaia, the Earth's soul, which, itself, is developing its personality and soulhood. The group dynamic that is the United States is a personality aspect of Gaia, as is the group dynamic that is Canada and the group dynamic that is Greenland, and the group dynamic that is each nation. The individual human souls that participate in the evolution of these aspects of Gaia form these group energy dynamics and, at the same time, their own developments are served by the karmic energy properties of these nations.

Consider the United States, for example, as simply one unit of energy that is evolving with a particular consciousness. The individual souls that pass through this collective consciousness expand it, create actions, create thought forms, create causes and effects, and that is how it accumulates karma. The relationship of these souls to their nation is like that of cells to a body. Your consciousness affects every cell in your body, and every cell in your body affects your consciousness. There is a mutuality. Each individual in the collective consciousness that is called the United States can be thought of as a cell in that nation, in dialogue.

The Earth school and the Earth are not the same. The Earth is a planet. With or without humanity, it would be. The purpose of the planet is double, so to speak. It has its own evolution, and part of its evolution includes the housing of a species called human. The Earth has agreed to interact with the human species, and to allow the development of this species to merge with its own consciousness. Part of this agreement can be understood as an agreement that matter will be cocreated upon this planet with the consciousness of the Earth. Since the Earth now has creative residents, it responds to their energy. Our species and the Earth form a mutual response system. This happens in the same way that Nature exists, and is also a cocreative adventure.

As you continue to move outward through the layers of your reality, they become more and more impersonal. The next layer of your reality is your race. If you are black, you—your soul—has chosen to participate in the evolution of what it is to be a black human. Your experiences of exhilaration, anger, wisdom, or kindness help to shape this impersonal energy dynamic.

The next layer is your sex. If you are female, you have chosen to participate in the evolution of femininity within the human species.

If you look upon this structure as an inverted pyramid, with your personal reality at the bottom, and each layer of your reality above your personal reality as more inclusive and more impersonal, the uppermost layer, the broadest and most impersonal layer, is humanity, the experience of being human.

As an individual you participate in group experiences simultaneously with being an individual, just as you can simultaneously be a man, a father, and a husband, or a woman, a wife, and a mother. These experiences are all simultaneous. Some of them are collective, and some of them are individual. You can have an individual experience as a father, for example, and an occupation as a baseball player with a team. There you participate in a group energy system.

You contribute to the creation and the evolution of each of the collective consciousness in which you participate. If a person is French, he or she contributes to the evolution of the group consciousness that is called French. If a person is Catholic, he or she contributes to the group consciousness that is called Catholic.

In other words, the dynamic of creating reality operates at more than one level. While you are here you participate in the creation of both personal reality and impersonal reality. Just as you can participate in the creation of a building that will remain long after you are gone, you participate in the evolution of group energy dynamics that will remain after you are gone.

Creating a building is a group effort. Several souls participate in the construction of that reality. It is built with group energy, and not with just individual energy. Therefore, it has an existence that is independent of each of the individuals that built it. In the same way, you are participating in the evolution of the United States, yet when you die, this place called the United States will continue.

You are connected in layers and through layers to your experience. As you advance from the individual experience of your own life into the larger experience of the family of which you are a part, and beyond, you move into dynamics of group energy. The group dynamic of the family is part of the larger group dynamic of the community, which is part of the larger group dynamic of the nation. Group dynamics advance through the system and the entire system—the entire inverted pyramid—is the soul of the human species.

The soul of the human species is sometimes called the collective unconscious, but it is not that. It is the soul of humankind. Your soul is a miniature of the soul of the human species. It is a micro of a macro. It has as much individual energy and power. As part of the micro, you have all the power of the macro calibrated to an individual form of certain frequencies. You form collective energies that help the whole evolve, although they are not themselves souls, and do not have souls. In between the micro and the macro are the various experiences afforded the individual human soul learning within a group, participating in group evolution, such as the evolution of your country, your religion, and the individual personal experiences that comprise the human experience.

As you move down from the top layer of the inverted

pyramid to the layer beneath it, your experience reduces from being a part of the whole of human evolution to being a part of the evolution of male or female energy. In the next layer down, you become part of the evolution of caucasian, or negro, or mongoloid. In the next layer down you are part of the evolution of the energy field of the United States. In the next layer down you are part of the evolution of an individual whose experiences will include an aspect that participates in the evolution of military, an aspect that participates in the evolution of teacher, an aspect that participates in the evolution of father, and so on. Layer by layer, that is what the reality of each individual looks like.

From the top layer, which is all humanity, all humanness, each layer downward locates you more individually and more specifically. The most impersonal consciousness, the human species, is the first layer. This consciousness then takes on personal attributes. It is personal that you are part of the United States. It is personal that you are a white male part of the United States, or a brown female part. These are parts of your personal experience and characteristics that serve the evolution of the whole.

A university, by analogy, is a group dynamic. Each of the schools of a university—undergraduate, business, medicine, law—is also a group energy system, a less inclusive collective of group energy of souls in evolution. What happens within the schools affects the whole of the university itself. Then within a particular school there is the experience of a certain class, which is more personal, and after that the experience of the student himself or herself, which is intimately personal.

The reality of each individual is created by his or her intentions and the intentions of others. What we think of as a physical reality that we share is an intermingling, or a formation, a massive overlay of appropriate realities. It is a fluid massive consciousness in which each of us exists independently of each other and yet coexists interdependently with each other.

What we, as a species and as individuals, are now becoming aware of is the effect of consciousness on this process.*

---

* To learn how to apply what you have learned in this chapter and deepen your experiences, see the Chapter 7 Study Guide on page 278.

— 8 —

Intention II

Y ou are the product of the karma of your soul. The dispositions, aptitudes, and attitudes that you were born with serve the learning of your soul. As your soul learns the lessons that it must learn to balance its energy, those characteristics become unnecessary, and are replaced by others. This is how you grow. As you come to realize, for example, that anger leads nowhere, your anger begins to disappear and you move into a more integrated and mature orientation toward your experiences. What once angered you now brings forth different responses.

Until you become aware of the effects of your anger, you continue to be an angry person. If you do not reach this awareness by the time you return home, your soul will continue this lesson through the experiences of another lifetime. It will incarnate another personality with aspects that are similar to your own. What is not learned in each lifetime is carried over into other lifetimes, along with new lessons that arise for the soul to learn, new karmic obligations that result from the responses of its personality to the situations that it encounters. The lessons that the soul has learned also are brought forward into other lifetimes, and this is how the soul evolves. Personalities mature in time, and the soul evolves in eternity.

Your dispositions, aptitudes, and attitudes reflect your intentions. If you are angry, fearful, resentful, or vengeful, your intention is to keep people at a distance. The human emotional spectrum can be broken down into two basic elements: love and fear. Anger, resentment, and vengeance are expressions of fear, as are guilt, regret, embarrassment, shame, and sorrow. These are lower-frequency currents of energy. They produce feelings of depletion, weakness, inability to cope, and exhaustion. The highest-frequency current, the highest energy current, is love. It produces buoyancy, radiance, lightness, and joy.

Your intentions create the reality that you experience. Until you become aware of this, it happens unconsciously. Therefore, be mindful of what you project. That is the first step toward authentic power.

You may seek companionship and warmth, for example, but if your unconscious intention is to keep people at a distance, the experiences of separation and pain will surface again and again until you come to understand that you, yourself, are creating them. Eventually, you will choose to create harmony and love. You will choose to draw to you the highest-frequency currents that each situation has to offer. Eventually, you will come to understand that love heals everything, and love is all there is.

This journey may take many lifetimes, but you will complete it. It is impossible not to complete it. It is not a question of if but of when. Every situation that you create serves this purpose. Every experience that you encounter serves this purpose.

The healing journey of the human soul through its incarnations into the physical arena is a process of cycles of creation:

$$Karma \rightarrow personality \rightarrow intentions + Energy \rightarrow$$
$$experiences \rightarrow reactions \rightarrow Karma \rightarrow etc.$$

The karma of the soul determines the characteristics of the personality. It determines the physical, emotional, psychological, and spiritual circumstances into which the personality is born. It determines the ways that the personality is prone to understand its experiences. It determines the intentions with which the personality will shape its reality. These intentions create the reality that provides the soul, at each moment, with the experiences that are necessary for the balancing of its energy, and the personality with the clearest choice between learning through wisdom or learning through doubt and fear. Through these intentions the personality shapes the Light that is flowing through it into the reality that is optimal for its growth, for the evolution of its soul.

The reactions of the personality to the experiences that it has created create more karma. Reactions express intentions. They determine the experiences that will be created next, and the reactions of the personality to those experiences create more karma, and so forth, until the soul releases that personality and body.

When the soul returns to its home, what has been accumulated in that lifetime is assessed with the loving assistance of its Teachers and guides. The new lessons that have emerged to be learned, the new karmic obligations that must be paid, are seen. The experiences of the incarnation just completed are reviewed in the fullness of understanding. Its mysteries are mysteries no more. Their causes, their reasons, and their contributions to the evolution of the soul, and to the evolution of the souls with whom the soul shared its life, are revealed. What has been balanced, what has been learned, brings the soul ever closer to its healing, to its integration and wholeness.

If the soul sees that it is necessary, it will choose, also with the help of its Teachers and guides, another incarnation. It will draw to itself the guides and Teachers that are appropriate to what it seeks to accomplish. It will consult with other souls whose evolution, like its own, will be mutually served by interactions within the physical arena. Then it will undertake again the massive, voluntary reduction of its energy, the infusion of its energy into matter, the calibration of its energy to an appropriate scale and range of frequencies, that is an incarnation into the learning environment of the Earth school, and the process begins again.

The world as we know it has been built without a consciousness of soul. It has been built with the consciousness of the personality. Everything within our world reflects personality energy. We believe that what we can see and smell and touch and feel and taste is all there is to the world. We believe that we are not responsible for the consequences of our actions. We act as though we are not affected when we take and take and take. We strive for external power and in that striving create a destructive competition.

The introduction of consciousness into the cyclic process of creation through which the soul evolves permits the creation of a world that is built upon the consciousness of the soul, a world that reflects the values and perceptions and experiences of the soul. It allows you to bring the energy of your soul consciously into the physical environment. It allows the consciousness of the sacred to fuse with physical matter.

The world in which we live has been created unconsciously by unconscious intentions. Every intention sets energy into motion whether you are conscious of it or not. You create in each moment. Each word that you speak carries consciousness—more than that, carries intelligence—and, therefore, is an intention that shapes Light.

When you speak of a "marriage," for example, you invoke

a particular consciousness, a particular energy. When two people marry, they become "husband" and "wife." "Husband" means the master of a house, the head of a household, a manager. "Wife" means a woman who is joined to a man in marriage, a hostess of a household. Sometimes it means a woman of humble rank. The relationship between a husband and a wife is not equal. When two people "marry," and think and speak of themselves as "husband" and "wife," they enter into these consciousnesses and intelligences.

In other words, the archetypical structure of "marriage" can be thought of as a planet. When two souls marry, they fall into the orbit, or gravitational field, of this planet and, therefore, despite their own individual intentions, they take on the characteristics of this planet called "marriage." They become part of the evolution of the structure itself through their own participation in a marriage.

An archetype is a collective human idea. The archetype of marriage was designed to assist physical survival. When two people marry, they participate in an energy dynamic in which they merge their lives in order to help each other survive physically. The archetype of marriage is no longer functional. It is being replaced with a new archetype that is designed to assist spiritual growth. This is the archetype of spiritual, or sacred, partnership.

The underlying premise of a spiritual partnership is a sacred commitment between the partners to assist each other's spiritual growth. Spiritual partners recognize their equality. Spiritual partners are able to distinguish personality from soul, and, therefore, they are able to discuss the dynamics between them, their interactions, on a less emotionally bound ground than husbands and wives. That ground does not exist within the consciousness of marriage. It exists only within the consciousness of spiritual partnership because spiritual partners are able to see clearly that there is indeed a deeper reason why they are together, and that that reason has a great deal to do with the evolution of their souls.

Because spiritual, or sacred, partners can see from this perspective, they engage in a very different dynamic than do husbands and wives. The conscious evolution of the soul is not part of the structural dynamic of marriage. It does not exist within that evolution because when the evolutionary archetype of marriage was created for our species, the dynamic of conscious spiritual growth was far too mature a concept to be included. What makes a spiritual, or sacred, partnership is that the souls within the partnership understand that they are together in a committed relationship, but the commitment is not to physical security. It is rather to be with each other's physical lives as they reflect spiritual consciousness.

The bond between spiritual partners exists as real as it does in marriage, but for significantly different reasons. Spiritual partners are not together in order to quell each other's financial fears or because they can produce a house in the suburbs and that entire conceptual framework. The understanding or consciousness that spiritual partners bring to their commitment is different, and, therefore, their commitment is dynamically different. The commitment of spiritual partners is to each other's spiritual growth, recognizing that that is what each of them is doing on Earth, and that everything serves that.

Spiritual partners bond with an understanding that they are together because it is appropriate for their souls to grow together. They recognize that their growth may take them to the end of their days in this incarnation and beyond, or it may take them to six months. They cannot say that they will be together forever. The duration of their partnership is determined by how long it is appropriate for their evolution to be together. All of the vows that a human being can take cannot prevent the spiritual path from exploding through and breaking those vows if the spirit must move on. It is appropriate for spiritual partners to remain together only as long as they grow together.

Spiritual partnership is a much freer and more spiritually accurate dynamic than marriage because spiritual partners come together from a position of spirit and consciousness. How spiritual partners merge and move their concept of partnership is a matter of free will. So long as they recognize that they bring the consequences of their choices into their partnership, and know the full extent of their choices, that is what influences the manner and direction that the partnership goes.

Spiritual partners commit to a growing dynamic. Their commitment is truly a promise toward their own growth, to their own spiritual survival and enhancement, and not to their physical.

The archetype of spiritual partnership is new to the human experience. Because there is not yet a social convention for spiritual partnership, spiritual partners may decide that the convention of marriage, reinterpreted to meet their needs, is the most appropriate physical expression of their bond. These souls infuse the archetype of marriage with the energy of the archetype of spiritual partnership, as do marriage partners who have discovered in their togetherness that their bond is actually one of commitment to mutual spiritual growth rather than to physical survival or security or comfort.

Just as external power is no longer appropriate to our evolution, the archetype of marriage is no longer appropriate. This does not mean that the institution of marriage will disappear overnight. Marriages will continue to exist, but marriages that succeed will only succeed with the consciousness of spiritual partnership. The partners in these marriages contribute through their participation in them to the archetype of spiritual partnership.

When you bring the consciousness of your soul to your intention-setting process, when you choose to align yourself with your soul instead of with your personality, you create a reality that reflects your soul rather than your personality. When you look upon the experiences of your life as karmic necessities, when you respond to your experiences as the products of an impersonal energy dynamic rather than the products of particular interactions, you bring the wisdom of your soul into your reality. When you choose to respond to life's difficulties with compassion and love instead of fear and doubt, you create a "heaven on Earth"—you bring the aspects of a more balanced and harmonious level of reality into physical being.

The introduction of consciousness into the cyclical processes of creation at the point of intention, and at the point of reaction, allows choice. It permits the selection of alternatives. It brings consciousness to the process of evolution. Your intention and attention shape your experiences. What you intend, through the density of matter, through the densest level of Light, becomes your reality. Where your attention goes, you go.

If you attend to the negative aspects of life, if you choose to focus your attention on the weaknesses of others, on their faults and shortcomings, you draw to yourself the lower-frequency energy currents of disdain, anger, and hatred. You put distance between yourself and others. You create obstacles to your loving. Your energy and influence move slowly through the realm of the personality, the arena of time and space and matter. If you direct your energy into criticism of others with the intention to disempower them, you create negative karma.

If you choose to focus your attention on the strengths of others, on the virtues of others, on that part of others that strives for the highest, you run through your system the higher-frequency currents of appreciation, acceptance, and love. Your energy and influence radiate instantaneously from soul to soul. You become an effective instrument of constructive change. If your intention is to align your personality with your soul, and if you focus your attention upon those perceptions that bring to you in each situation the highest-frequency currents of energy, you move toward authentic empowerment.

As you come to recognize the power of your consciousness, that what is behind your eyes, so to speak, holds more power than what appears in front of them, your inner and outer perceptions change. You cannot become compassionate with yourself without becoming compassionate with others, or with others without becoming compassionate with yourself. When you are compassionate with yourself and others, your world becomes compassionate. You draw to yourself other souls of like frequency, and with them you create, through your intentions and your actions and your interactions, a compassionate world.

As you come to seek and see the virtues and strengths and nobilities of others, you begin to seek and see them in yourself also. As you draw to yourself the highest-frequency currents of each situation, you radiate that frequency of consciousness, and change the situation. You become more and more and more consciously a being of Light.

To become aware of the relationship between your consciousness and physical reality is to become aware of the law of karma, to see it in action. What you intend is what you become. If you intend to take as much from life and others as you can, if your thoughts are of taking instead of giving, you create a reality that reflects your intentions. You draw to yourself souls of like frequency, and together you create a

taking reality. Your experiences then reflect your own orientation, and validate it. You see the people around you as
personalities who take, rather than personalities who give.
You do not trust them, and they do not trust you.

The creative dynamic of intention, the relationship between intention and experience, underlies quantum physics,
our species' most profound attempt to comprehend physical
phenomena from the perspective of the five-sensory personality. Quantum physics was born of an intense and cumula-
tive effort to understand the nature of physical light.

It is possible to build a device that reveals the wave-like
nature of light, that causes light to produce phenomena that
can only be produced by waves. It is also possible to make
a device that detects particles of light, as though they were
tiny pellets, and to measure the force of the impact of each
particle. Yet, it is not possible for light to be described as a
wave phenomenon and a particle phenomenon at the same
time. In other words, it is not possible to describe the nature
of light—literally, the shape of physical light—apart from
the experimental apparatus that is used to determine it, and
this depends upon the intention of the experimenter.

The scientific accomplishments of our species reflect our
awareness as a species of nonphysical dynamics as they unfold within the arena of matter and time, within the realm
of the five-sensory personality. The dependency of the form
of physical light upon the intention of the experimenter reflects in a limited but accurate manner the dependency of
the form of nonphysical Light upon the intentions of the

soul that shape it, just as the nature of physical light itself reflects in a limited but essentially accurate way the nature of the Light of the Universe.

The creation of physical experience through intention, the infusion of Light into form, energy into matter, soul into body, are all the same. The distance between you and your understanding of the creation of matter from energy is equal to the distance that exists between the awareness of your personality and the energy of your soul. The dynamic of soul and personality is the same dynamic as energy converted into matter. The system is identical. Your body is your conscious matter. Your personality is the energy of your soul converted to matter. If it is unaware, it is the splinteredness that is transmitted. If it is aware, it begins to become whole.

The dynamic of soul-to-personality, energy-to-matter, lies at the heart of our creation mythology, the story of Paradise. Are you not metaphorically within a Garden of Eden, so to speak, your own creative reality, within which you choose each day how you will create your reality with the male-female principle inside of you, the Adam and Eve principle, with the Tree representing your personal energy system, your own cord of knowledge? How will you use your power? Will you create Paradise or be Cast Out, as it were?

The challenge to each human is creation.

Will you create with reverence, or with neglect?*

---

* To learn how to apply what you have learned in this chapter and deepen your experiences, see the Chapter 8 Study Guide on page 283.

RESPONSIBILITY

— 9 —

Choice

The center of the evolutionary process is choice. It is the engine of our evolution. Each choice that you make is a choice of intention. You may choose to remain silent in a particular situation, for example, and that action may serve the intention of penalizing, sharing compassion, extracting vengeance, showing patience, or loving. You may choose to speak forcefully, and that action may serve any of the same intentions. What you choose, with each action and each thought, is an intention, a quality of consciousness that you bring to your action or your thought.

The splintered personality has several, or many, aspects. One aspect may be loving and patient, another may be vindictive, another charitable, and another selfish. Each of these aspects has its own values and goals. If you are not conscious of all of the different parts of yourself, the part of yourself that is the strongest will win out over the other parts. Its intention will be the one that the personality uses to create its reality. The charitable part of you, for example, may want to see the burglar that was caught in your house given another chance, but if the vindictive part of you is stronger, you will, perhaps with mixed feelings, press for his or her arrest.

You cannot choose your intentions consciously until you become conscious of each of the different aspects of yourself. If you are not conscious of each part of yourself, you will have the experience of wanting to say, or to intend, one thing, and finding yourself saying or intending something else. You will want your life to move in one direction, and find that it is moving in another. You will desire to release a painful pattern from your experience, and see it reappear yet again.

It is not easy for a splintered personality to become whole because only some parts of a splintered personality seek wholeness. The other parts, because they are not as responsible, or caring, or compassionate as the parts that seek wholeness, pull the other way. They seek to create what satisfies them, what they have become accustomed to. These parts of the personality are often strong and well established. The splintered personality must always choose between opposing parts of itself. This is the backbone situation of our evolution. This is the foundational situation—the point of choice.

The choice of intention is also the choice of karmic path.

If you speak or act from anger, for example, you create the karma of anger. If you speak or act with compassion, you create the karma of compassion, and a different path opens before you. This happens whether you are aware of the different parts of yourself or not, whether even you are aware of the choices that you make at each moment. Unconscious evolution through the density of physical matter, through the experiences that are created unconsciously by unconscious intentions, has been the way of our species to now. This is the unconscious road to authentic empowerment.

Conscious evolution through responsible choice is the accelerated way of evolution of the multisensory personality, and the five-sensory personality that is becoming multisensory. Responsible choice is the conscious road to authentic empowerment.

What is responsible choice?

As you follow your feelings, you become aware of the different parts of yourself, and the different things that they want. You cannot have all of them at once because many of them conflict. The part of you that wants more money and a bigger house conflicts with the part of you that suffers with the poor and hungry. The part of you that reaches out with compassion toward the beauty in others conflicts with the part of you that wants to use others for your own benefit or gratification. When you satisfy one part of yourself, the needs of another go unsatisfied. The fulfillment of one part of you creates anguish in another, or others, and you are torn.

Just as the experimenter in quantum physics cannot produce the experience of waves from physical light and the experience of particles from physical light at the same time, and must choose which experience he or she will create, so you, also, as you shape nonphysical Light must choose which experience you will create.

As you become conscious of the different parts of your personality, you become able to experience consciously the forces within you that compete for expression, that lay claim to the single intention that will be yours at each moment, that will shape your reality. When you enter these dynamics consciously, you create for yourself the ability to choose consciously among the forces within you, to choose where and how you will focus your energy.

The choice not to choose is the choice to remain unconscious and, therefore, to wield power irresponsibly. Awareness of the splintered personality and of its need for integration brings with it the need for conscious choice. Each decision requires that you choose which parts of yourself you want to cultivate, and which parts you want to release.

A responsible choice is a choice that takes into account the consequences of each of your choices. In order to make a responsible choice you must ask yourself, for each choice that you are considering, "What will this produce? Do I really want to create that? Am I ready to accept all of the consequences of this choice?" Project yourself into the probable future that will unfold with each choice that you are considering. Do this not with the energy of intention, but simply to test the water, to get the feel for what you are considering creating. See how you feel. Ask yourself, "Is this what I really want?" and then decide. When you take the consequences of your choice into your decision, and when you choose to remain conscious, that is a responsible choice.

Only through responsible choice can you choose consciously to cultivate and nourish the needs of your soul, and to challenge and release the wants of your personality. This is the choice of clarity and wisdom, the choice of conscious transformation. It is the choice of the higher-frequency energy currents of love, forgiveness, and compassion. It is the choice to follow the voice of your higher self, your soul. It is the decision to open yourself to the guidance and assistance of your guides and Teachers. It is the path that leads consciously to authentic power.

How does this happen?

You may be aware that deceiving another person is not in alignment with your soul, but decide to do that anyway in order to gain a profit, or save a relationship that you are not yet ready to lose. You may know that the path of compassion is to share your thoughts and actions, and yet decide not to share them because you think that would cost you money, or security. When you choose the energy of your soul—when you choose to create with the intentions of love, forgiveness, humbleness, and clarity—you gain power. When you choose to learn through wisdom, you gain power. When you choose to create with the energy of your personality, with anger, jealousy, or fear—when you choose to learn through fear and doubt—you lose power. You gain or lose power, therefore, according to the choices that you make.

The personality is interested in itself. It likes thrills, so to speak. It is not necessarily responsible nor caring nor loving. The soul is the energy of Universal love, wisdom, and compassion. It creates with these energies. The personality understands power as external; it perceives in terms of competition, threats, and gains and losses that are measured against those of others. When you align yourself with your personality, you give power to the realm of the five senses, to external circumstances and objects. You disempower yourself. As you grow aware of your spiritual self and origin, your immortalness, and you choose and live according to that first, and the physical second, you close the gap that exists between the personality and the soul. You begin to experience authentic power.

When you interact in terms of the perceptions of your personality, in terms of your five senses, there is an illusion that you do not see. A disagreement between two friends, for example, is not so much a disagreement as aspects of each surfacing in order to be healed. If they were not souls in agreement, they would not be together at all. If a father longs to be at the birth of his son, for example, but circumstances take him elsewhere, the perception that he is elsewhere is an illusion. He is with his son. As the personality becomes whole and empowered, it becomes content to let the illusion play.

This is the creation of the dynamic of the soul whereby,

no matter what situation it is in, it creates the best of all worlds from the power that it draws to the situation. From the perception of the personality, it is not possible to see clearly those human beings who, from the outside, appear to be making foolish decisions, or to be unaware of their environment, when in truth they are simply drinking from the finest nectar of their environment and are totally content to let the illusion play.

The splintered personality is not content. The contentment that it feels in one moment is replaced by anger or fear or envy in the next moment as conflicting aspects of itself struggle with each other. Your responses to the struggles between the conflicting aspects of yourself determine the way that you will evolve, consciously or unconsciously, through the experience of negative karma or positive, through fear and doubt or through wisdom. Your struggles themselves do not create karma or determine the way that you will evolve, only your responses to them.

If your struggle with the conflicting parts of yourself is conscious, you are able to choose consciously the response that will create the karma that you desire. You will be able to bring to bear upon your decision an awareness of what lies behind each choice, and the consequences of each choice, and choose accordingly. When you enter into your decision-making dynamic consciously, you insert your will consciously into the creative cycle through which your soul evolves, and you enter consciously into your own evolution.

This requires effort, but is it really more difficult than

living through the consequences that follow a decision to act in anger, or selfishness, or fear when you know that with each decision to act without compassion you yourself will experience the discord, or fear, or anguish that you create in another? Is it not worth the effort to project yourself ahead into the probable consequences of each of your actions, at each point of choice, and see how you will feel in each instance, how comfortable you will be with each of the consequences, if doing that will allow you to harvest love, compassion, and authentic power?

The effort that you apply to each decision to align yourself with your soul is rewarded many times. The part of yourself that reaches toward Light may not be the strongest part of you at the moment that you choose to journey toward authentic power consciously, at the moment that you choose the vertical path, but it is the part that the Universe backs.

When it becomes necessary, for example, for the physical, emotional body of a person to heal, a dramatic shift in nutrition is often required wherein a person must release every one of his or her eating habits and take on the habits of eating certain foods that are much higher in vibration. Ninety percent of the person's personality may not want to do that, but the ten percent that is choosing that path for the sake of health and wholeness has more power ultimately than the ninety percent that is fighting to remain where it is and have its own way, because the Universe backs that ten percent and not the ninety percent.

Think in terms of what it means to make decisions and try to cause the rest of you to fall into alignment with them, of responsible choice, and as you move into the healing of who you are and the conscious journey toward what it is you want, recognize that the Universe backs the part of you that is of clearest intention.

You are constantly receiving guidance and assistance from your guides and Teachers, and from the Universe itself. When you choose consciously to move toward the energy of your soul, you invite that guidance. When you ask the Universe to bless you in your effort to align yourself with your soul, you open a passageway between yourself and your guides and Teachers. You assist their efforts to assist you. You invoke the power of the nonphysical world. That is what a blessing is: the opening of a passageway between you and nonphysical guidance.

A personality that is conscious of its splinteredness, and struggles consciously to become whole, does not need to create negative karma in order to evolve, in order to learn to create responsibility, in order to acquire authentic power. When you struggle consciously with a choice between the wants of your personality and the needs of your soul, you enter a dynamic through which you are enabled to evolve without creating negative karma. That is the dynamic of temptation.

What is temptation?

Temptation is the Universe's compassionate way of allowing you to run through what would be a harmful negative karmic dynamic if you were to allow it to become physically manifest. It is the energy through which your soul is given the gracious opportunity to have a dry run at a life lesson, at a situation that, if you can see clearly, can be removed and healed within the confines of your private world of energy and not spill into a larger energy field of other souls. Temptation is a dress rehearsal for a karmic experience of negativity.

The entire dynamic of temptation is the compassionate way of allowing you to see your potential pitfalls, and cleanse yourself before you can affect the lives of others. It is a form of decoy in which the negativity is compassionately drawn from you, if you can see that before you create karma. As you respond to the decoy, you cleanse yourself by becoming aware and not having to actually live through the experience. You cleanse yourself without creating karma and interaction with other souls. How exquisite is temptation. It is the magnet which draws your awareness to that which would create negative karma if it were allowed to remain unconscious.

In other words, temptation is a thought form that is designed to draw possible negativity from the human energy system without harming others. The soul understands that. Left to its own device it would operate completely within the human energy system, without spilling over and contaminating the collective conscious.

Temptations are not traps. Each temptation is an opportunity through which the soul is able to learn without creating karma, to evolve directly through conscious choice.

The dynamic of temptation is the energy of what might be thought of as the challenging dynamic of the human experience, as the Luciferic principle. It serves the purpose of assisting the evolution of power.

Lucifer means "Light bringer." Temptation, the Luciferic principle, is that dynamic through which each soul is graciously offered the opportunity to challenge those parts of itself that resist Light. The Luciferic energy is represented in the Garden of Eden story by a snake, by the idea of a presence other than human that could tempt, but, literally, could not have dominion over the human being. The Luciferic energy tempts you, tempts the level of human being that is mortal, that is five-sensory, but the snake cannot destroy the soul. It can merely threaten that part of you that becomes too linked to the physical. The snake is of the Earth. When you are too close to the Earth, when you find yourself honoring the gods of the Earth, and make Earth your god and master, then so, too, you shall be bitten.

The Light-bringing energy, the Luciferic energy, that tempted the person Jesus of Nazareth who became the Christ, and that tempted the person Siddhartha Gautama who became the Buddha, is the same energy that tempts you. It tempts the accountant to steal, the student to cheat, the spouse to adultery, the human being to external power. It opposes the Light of your immortal soul to the physical light of your personality. It sets before you the vertical path and the horizontal path. What is the nature of transformation? It is the compassionate way of temptation.

Temptation is the gracious way of introducing each indi-

vidual to his or her power. When you are seduced or threatened by external circumstances, you lose power. They gain
power over you. With each choice that you make to align
yourself with the energy of your soul, you empower yourself. This is how authentic power is acquired. It is built up
step by step, choice by choice. It cannot be meditated or
prayed into being. It must be earned.

When you choose to release anger, for example, you
create an energy template around which your experiences
will form. This energy pattern will draw to the surface the
anger within you in order that you can release it. When you
choose to challenge and to release a negative aspect of yourself, that aspect comes to the foreground. Everything starts
to serve that purpose. Your dreams show you the archetypical dynamics of your anger. You find yourself continually in
situations that generate anger within you. Your life appears
to be distorted around anger, because that is the aspect of
yourself that you have chosen to challenge, and the Universe
has responded to your choice with compassion.

When you consciously invoke growing, consciously invoke wisdom, you consciously invoke the parts of yourself
that are not whole to come into the foreground of your life.
With each recurrence of anger, or jealousy, or fear, you are
given the choice to challenge it, or to give in to it. Each
time you challenge it, it loses power and you gain power.
Each time you are tempted to become angry, or jealous, or
fearful, and you challenge that feeling, you empower yourself. There would be no accumulation of strength inside if

the choices that you make did not require discipline and intention.

If you decide that you cannot beat a temptation, what you are really doing is giving yourself permission to be irresponsible. The desires and impulses that you feel that you cannot resist, that you lack the power to overcome, are your addictions. Addictions are the wants of the parts of your personality that are very strong and resistant to the energy of your soul. They are those aspects of your personality, of your soul incarnate, that are most in need of healing. They are your greatest inadequacies.

Your addiction may be to food, or drugs, or anger, or sex. You may have more than one addiction. In each instance, you cannot release the addiction until you understand the dynamic that underlies it. Beneath every addiction is the perception of power as external, as the ability to control and use the environment or others. Beneath every addiction is an issue of power.

The journey to the soul begins with understanding that we are drawn automatically as a species to come to terms with power. Each human being is experiencing the causes and effects of his or her choices, his or her desires to fill in the empty, powerless places within him or her. This dynamic can be described in terms of an insecure humanity, but that is just the obvious. The mechanism at work is the journey toward genuine, authentic empowerment.

This is why each human being struggles so deeply with power: the lack of it, the acquisition of it, what it is really, how one should have it. Underlying every crisis, emotional, spiritual, physical, and psychological, is the issue of power. Depending upon the lens that you wear to interpret your crisis, you will either step closer to your soul or closer to the Earth.

The journey to wholeness requires that you look honestly, openly, and with courage into yourself, into the dynamics that lie behind what you feel, what you perceive, what you value, and how you act. It is a journey through your defenses and beyond so that you can experience consciously the nature of your personality, face what it has produced in your life, and choose to change that.*

---

* To learn how to apply what you have learned in this chapter and deepen your experiences, see the Chapter 9 Study Guide on page 288.

— 10 —

Addiction

Y ou cannot begin the work of releasing an addiction until
you can acknowledge that you are addicted. Until you realize
that you have an addiction, it is not possible to diminish its
power. The personality rationalizes its addictions. It dresses
them in attractive clothing. It presents them to itself and others as desirable or beneficial. A person who is addicted to alcohol, for example, will say to herself or himself, or to others,
that drunkenness is a way of loosening up, of relaxing after a
tense day, of having fun, and, therefore, it is constructive. A
person who is addicted to sex will say to herself or himself,
or to others, that random sexual encounters are expressions
of closeness, or love, that they reflect an evolved and liberated
perception, and, therefore, they are desirable.

Recognition of your own addictions requires inner work. It requires that you look clearly at the places where you lose power in your life, where you are controlled by external circumstances. It requires going through your defenses. Even when striving for clarity, or when outer circumstances—such as an injury caused by driving drunk, or a marriage wrecked by promiscuity—provide evidence of an addiction, the personality often clings to a perception of its addiction as a mere problem, initially, as a small problem, then as a bigger problem, and then as a significant problem.

Why does the personality resist acknowledging its addictions?

Acknowledging an addiction, accepting that you have an addiction, is acknowledgment that a part of you is out of control. The personality resists acknowledging its addictions because that forces it to choose to leave a part of itself out of control, or to do something about it. Once an addiction has been acknowledged, it cannot be ignored, and it cannot be released without changing your life, without changing your self-image, without changing your entire perceptual and conceptual framework. We do not want to do that because it is our nature to resist change. Therefore, we resist acknowledging our addictions.

An addiction is not merely an attraction. It is natural for males and females to admire each other, for example, and to feel a warmth and attraction toward each other. An addiction is more than that. An addiction is characterized by magnetism and fear. There is attraction plus fear, plus a jolt of energy that is out of proportion to the situation. Attractions are a pleasing part of life. They can be satisfied and left behind, but addictions cannot.

An addiction cannot be satiated. A sexual addiction, for example, cannot be satisfied by sex. This is the first clue that the dynamic that is involved in what appears to be a sexual addiction is not sexual, but that the experiences of addictive sexual attraction, or repulsion, serve a deeper dynamic.

An addiction can be anesthetized. A sexual addiction, for example, can be made dormant within a relationship by a fear of losing the security of the relationship, but it cannot be healed without a recognition that it is there, and an understanding of the dynamic that lies beneath it. Unless this takes place, it will break through the relationship, or the facade of monogamy, at those moments when the personality feels most insecure, or most threatened. At these times, the personality will feel a sexual attraction to others.

Sexual addictions are the most universal within our species because the issues of power are tied so directly to the learning of sexuality within the human structure. Sexuality and issues of power were created within our species to complement each other. That is why each human being who is sexually out of control actually has issues of power in which he or she is out of control with his or her own power. At heart, they are identical. A person cannot be in his or her own power center and be sexually out of control or dominated by the sexual energy current. These cannot exist simultaneously.

What is the dynamic behind sexual addiction?

The experience of addictive sexual attraction is a signal to the experiencer that in that moment he or she is experiencing powerlessness, and is desiring to feed upon a weaker soul. This is the dynamic beneath all addictions: the desire to prey upon a soul that is more shattered than oneself. This is as ugly to look at as it is to experience, but it is the central core of negativity within our species.

Sex without reverence, like business without reverence, and politics without reverence, and any activity that is done without reverence, reflects the same thing: one soul preying upon another weaker soul. The way out of a sexual addiction, therefore, is to remind yourself when you feel that attraction, that you are, in that moment, powerless, and desiring to prey upon a soul that is weaker than yourself.

In other words, when you are feeling the draw of a sexual addiction, consider simultaneously that you are in a mode of powerlessness that causes a desire to use others to surface within you. That desire feels like a sexual attraction. Remind yourself clearly of what it is that is being ignited in you. That does not mean that you do not physically feel a connection or an attraction, but, underneath it, what causes you to want to act is a different dynamic, one of powerlessness.

Allow this consciousness to penetrate deeply within you so that, at that point, if you want to act on your addiction, you need to walk through your own reality.

What does this mean?

If you are married, or in a monogamous relationship, remind yourself that acting upon your impulse may, or will, cost you your marriage, or your relationship. Ask yourself if what you want to do is worth that. If you are healthy, remind yourself that acting upon your impulse may cost you your health, because you do not know whether or not the partner that you have chosen carries a disease, such as AIDS. Ask yourself if what you want to do is worth that risk.

Remind yourself that the partner to whom you are most likely drawn is drawn equally to others, as are you, that he or she has no more feeling for you than you have for him or her. You can be assured that this is the case because the sexual attraction that you have felt for this person is a response in you of a weakness detection system, so to speak, that you have used to scan those around you. When it locates a person who is weak enough to be susceptible to you, to be seduced by you, it triggers within you the experience of sexual attraction. Will you advance your masculinity, or your femininity, by exploiting the weakness of this person? Will that gain you what you want to gain?

Remind yourself that you both have chosen to interact sexually in ways that do not ignite your feelings because, if your feelings were awakened, they would only let you know that the person you are drawn to is no more emotionally involved with you than you are with him or her. It is one thing to think that you are sexually involved with someone and not feeling anything. It is another to face that neither is your partner feeling anything for you.

Look closely at the dynamic in which you are involved, and you will see that when one soul seeks to prey upon a weaker soul, and a weaker soul responds, both souls are the weaker soul. Who preys upon whom? The logic of the five-sensory personality cannot grasp this, but the higher-order logic of the heart sees it clearly. Is there truly a difference when two consciousnesses are trying to link into a dynamic that ultimately will lead to balance when both have identical missing pieces? What causes the need to dominate, for example, is the same that causes the need to be submissive. It is merely the choice of which role the soul wishes to play in working out the identical struggle.

Enter into your own fear, into your own sense of wanting a drink, or sex with a different partner. Ask yourself to seriously review all of the times in your life that you thought you would gain so much from that, and face what you gained.

Hold on to the thought that you create your experiences. Your fear comes from the realization that a part of you is creating a reality that it wants, whether you want it or not, and the feeling that you are powerless to prevent it, but that is not so. This is critical to understand: Your addiction is not stronger than you. It is not stronger than who you want to be. Though it may feel that way, it can only win if you let it. Like any weakness, it is not stronger than the soul or the force of will. Its strength only indicates the amount of effort that needs to be applied toward the transition, toward making yourself whole in that area of your life.

Recognize that what you are doing when you fear that you will be tempted, and that you will not be able to resist the temptation, is creating a situation that will give you permission to act irresponsibly. Is it possible to create a test that you cannot pass? Yes. The experience of wanting to be tempted in order to test yourself is the act of creating an opportunity to act irresponsibly, to say to yourself, "I knew I couldn't do it, anyway," and give in to your addiction. The heart of making a temptation that is greater than you can resist is that you do not wish to be held responsible for your choice.

The greater the desire of your soul to heal your addiction, the greater will be the cost of keeping it. If you—if your soul—has chosen to heal an addiction now, you will find that the decision to maintain your addiction will cost you the things that you hold most dear. If that is your wife or your husband, your marriage will be placed in the balance against your addiction. If that is your career, your career will be placed in the balance.

This is not the doing of a cruel Universe or a malicious God. It is a compassionate response to your desire to heal, to become whole. It is the compassionate Universe saying to you that your inadequacies are so deep that the only thing that will stop you will be something of equal or greater value in opposition to your inadequacies. This is the same dynamic that is expressed in terms of space and time and matter by the second law of motion: "A change in the momentum (mass, direction of movement, and speed) of a body in motion is directly proportional to the force affecting the body in motion, and takes place in the direction that the force is acting." By the magnitude of the costs of your addiction you can measure the importance of healing it to your soul, and the strength of your own inner intention to do that.

Try to realize, and truly realize, that what stands between you and a different life are matters of responsible choice. In your moments of fear, what you are obscure about in your thinking is the power and magnitude of your own choice. Recognize what your own power of choice is. You are not at the mercy of your inadequacy. The intention that will empower you must come from a place within you that suggests that you are indeed able to make responsible choices and draw the power from them, that you can make choices that empower you and not disempower you, that you are capable of acts of wholeness. Test your power of choice because each time you choose otherwise you disengage the power of your addiction more and more and increase your personal power more and more.

As you work through your weaknesses, and you feel levels of addictive attraction, ask yourself the critical questions of the spirit: If, by following those impulses, do you increase your level of enlightenment? Does it bring you power of the genuine sort? Will it make you more loving? Will it make you more whole? Ask yourself these questions.

This is the way out of an addiction: Walk yourself through your reality step by step. Make yourself aware of the consequences of your decisions, and choose accordingly. When you feel in yourself the addictive attraction of sex, or alcohol, or drugs, or anything else, remember these words: You stand between the two worlds of your lesser self and your full self. Your lesser self is tempting and powerful because it is not as responsible and not as loving and not as disciplined, so it calls you. This other part of you is whole and more responsible and more caring and more empowered, but it demands of you the way of the enlightened spirit: conscious life. *Conscious* life. The other choice is unconscious permission to act without consciousness. It is tempting.

What choose you?

If your decision is to become whole, hold that decision. You will not be as tempted or as frightened as you think. Hold it and remind yourself again and again: You stand between your lesser self and your whole self. Choose with wisdom because the power is now fully in your hands. Do not underestimate the power of consciousness. As you live and make conscious choices each moment and each day you fill with strength and your lesser self disintegrates.

As you choose to empower yourself, the part of you that you challenge, the temptation that you challenge, will surface again and again. Each time that you challenge it, you gain power and it loses power. If you challenge an addiction to alcohol, for example, and you are drawn twelve times that very day to have a drink, challenge that energy each time. If you look upon each recurrence of attraction as a setback, or as an indication that your intention is not working, you choose the path of learning through fear and doubt. If you look upon each recurrence as an opportunity that is offered to you, in response to your intention, to release your inadequacy and to acquire power over it, you choose the path of learning through wisdom, for that is what it is.

The first time that you challenge your addiction, and the second, and the third, you may not feel that anything has been accomplished. Do you think that authentic power can be had so easily? As you hold to your intention, and as you choose again and again and again to become whole, you accumulate power, and the addiction that you thought could not be challenged will lose its power over you.

When you challenge an addiction, and choose to become whole, you align yourself with your nonphysical help. The work to be done is yours, but assistance is always there for you. The nonphysical world, the actions of your guides and Teachers, touches yours in many ways—the thought that brings power, the memory that reminds, the surprise occurrence that reinforces. There is much joy in the nonphysical world when a soul releases major negativity and the quality of its consciousness shifts upward into higher frequencies of Light. Therefore, do not suffer in aloneness. There is no such thing.

Look at yourself as someone who is reaching for healing, and at the complexity of what needs to be healed. Do not think that you exist alone without other human beings of equal complexity. All that the human experience is about is the journey toward wholeness. Therefore, you can look at each individual and rest assured that they are not whole. They are in process. Were they whole, they would not be physical upon our plane. In other words, you have the company of billions of souls.

When you have worked hard, take the time to appreciate what you have done. Do not always look at the distance that you have yet to travel. Join your nonphysical Teachers and guides in applauding what you have accomplished. This does not mean to relapse into your addiction. It means allowing yourself to rest when you need it, to recognize when you become exhausted, and to give yourself the grace of knowing that even the best of us get tired.

Understanding the dynamics behind your addiction is one thing. Actually making the emotional connection to discharge the need for it is another story. Your addiction is not insurmountable. It is not overwhelming. If it continues to appear that way to you, it is because deep in your heart you do not see yourself as able to release the addiction, even if you understand why you are drawn to it. If your addiction lingers, ask yourself if you really want to release it, because in your heart you do not.

Until you fill in the inadequacies within you, you will always have your addiction. In order to release your addiction, it is necessary to enter your inadequacies, to recognize that they are real, and to bring them into the light of consciousness to heal. It is necessary to look deeply into the parts of yourself that have such power to you, to look clearly at how deep they are within you, and to see them as honestly as you can. It may be that your addiction has provided you one of the few genuine pleasures of your life. What is more important to you, your wholeness, and your freedom, or the pleasures that you get from satisfying your addiction?

When you understand that your addiction results from an inadequacy, the question becomes how you will respond to your inadequacy—by reaching for another drink, or another sexual encounter, or by reaching inward for those things that fill the whole? Move into how strong the power of your addiction is, into how deeply you feel its attraction, and ask yourself if the time is really right for you to release this form of learning. That is for you to ask and answer. You may hear the guidance of your nonphysical Teachers, and feel that it offers you a path of higher wisdom, but at the same moment realize that you are not ready to take that path. You might decide that this is not the right time, that you are not yet strong enough to live a certain way. You might indeed have to face that.

Ultimately, you will take the higher path, but if you wish to put the journey off for a day or a week or seven lifetimes, that is sufficient. Your Teachers see from a perspective that does not include time. It is the depth of wisdom for you to know that you will eventually take the path of consciousness. If that is the path that you will eventually take, why wait? Yet, there are times when there is wisdom in waiting as the rest of you prepares for the journey. There is no shame in this decision.

The Universe does not judge. Eventually, you will come

to authentic empowerment. You will know the power of forgiveness, humbleness, clarity and love. You will evolve beyond the human experience, beyond the Earth school, beyond the learning environment of space and time and matter. You cannot not evolve. Everything in the Universe evolves. It is only a question of which way you will choose to learn as you evolve. This is always your choice, and there is always wisdom in each choice.

When you return home, when you leave your personality and body behind, you will leave behind your inadequacies, your fears and angers and jealousies. They do not, and cannot, exist within the realm of spirit. They are the experiences of the personality, of time and matter. You will once again enter the fullness of who you are. You will perceive with loving eyes and compassionate understanding the experiences of your life, including those that seemed so much to control you. You will see what purposes they served. You will survey what has been learned, and you will bring these things into your next incarnation.

If you choose to continue with your addiction, you choose to experience negative karma. You choose to create without compassion. You choose to be unconscious. You choose to learn through the experiences that your unconscious intentions create. You choose to learn through fear and doubt, because you fear your addiction and you doubt your power to challenge it successfully.

If you choose to challenge your addiction, to move consciously toward wholeness, you choose to learn through wisdom. You choose to create your experiences consciously, to align the perceptions and the energy of your personality with your soul. You choose to create within physical reality the reality that your soul wishes to create. You choose to allow your soul to move through you. You choose to allow Divinity to shape your world.

When you struggle with an addiction, you deal directly with the healing of your soul. You deal directly with the matter of your life. This is the work that is required to be done. As you face your deepest struggles, you reach for your highest goal. As you bring to light, heal, and release the deepest currents of negativity within you, you allow the energy of your soul to move directly into, and to shape, the experiences and events of physical reality, and thereby to accomplish unimpeded its tasks upon the Earth.

This is the work of evolution. It is the work that you were born to do.*

---

* To learn how to apply what you have learned in this chapter and deepen your experiences, see the Chapter 10 Study Guide on page 294.

— 11 —

Relationships

There are certain growing dynamics that can occur only within the dynamic of commitment. Without commitment you cannot learn to care for another person more than yourself. You cannot learn to value the growth of strength and clarity in another soul, even if that threatens the wants of your personality. When you release the wants of your personality in order to accommodate and encourage another's growth, you attune yourself to that person's soul. Without commitment, you cannot learn to see others as your soul sees them; as beautiful and powerful spirits of Light.

The archetype of spiritual partnership—partnership between equals for the purpose of spiritual growth—is emerging within our species. This is different from the archetype of marriage, which was designed to assist physical survival, and in which the partners do not necessarily see themselves as equals. When individuals enter into a marriage, the ability of each to survive physically is enhanced. They are more capable together of finding fire, shelter, food and water, and of defending themselves, than they are individually. The marriage archetype reflects the perception of power as external.

The archetype of spiritual partnership reflects the conscious journey of multisensory humans toward authentic power. Spiritual partners recognize the existence of the soul, and consciously seek to further its evolution. They recognize nonphysical dynamics at work within the world of time and matter. They see matter as the densest, or heaviest, level of Light that is continually being shaped and reshaped by the souls that share this sphere of learning. They consciously co-create their experiences with each other, with an alive Earth that loves Life very much, and with a compassionate Universe.

Communities, nations, and cultures—all of our collective creations—are built upon the values and perceptions of the five-sensory personality, the values that are reflected by the archetype of marriage. They are designed to serve the physical survival of our species. They also reflect the decisions of our species to learn through fear and doubt.

Our entire world is built upon the energy of the five-sensory personality that has chosen to learn through fear and doubt. Nations fear nations, races fear races, and the sexes fear each other. The exploration of physical reality, which is external power, could have been accomplished in a spirit of cooperation with, and appreciation of, the Earth. Instead, we chose as a species to explore it with a sense of domination and exploitation. This is the path of learning through fear and doubt, fear of the physical environment and doubt that we fit naturally into it.

Our world reflects the basic thought form that there is no afterlife, that in this lifetime the only thing that insures power is what can be had and gained. Sometimes we speak of an afterlife, but we do not really believe that after we leave the Earth we are still responsible for the choices that we have made upon the Earth or our choices would be very different.

Our species is no longer humble. It has no reverence. It is arrogant and filled with its own technology. It seduces itself constantly in terms of its illusions that it is in control, and so it creates chaos and still refuses to see that it is impossible for it to control. We take from the Earth and from each other. We destroy forests and oceans and atmosphere. We enslave each other, and torture and beat and humiliate and murder each other.

When the archetype of spiritual partnership—of individuals joined in equality for the purpose of spiritual growth—emerges at the level of community, it creates values and perceptions at that level that reflect those of the multisensory personality. Just as individuals that bond in spiritual partnership and choose to express their bond through the convention of marriage infuse the energy of spiritual partnership into the archetype of marriage, and thereby create new values and behaviors within marriage, individuals that join in spiritual partnership at the level of organization, city, nation, race, and sex infuse the collective consciousnesses of these levels with the energy of spiritual partnership, and create new values and behaviors at these levels.

The evolutionary process that occurs at the level of the individual is the same process that occurs at each level of interaction between individuals. When an individual invokes the energy of the archetype of spiritual partnership, not only the partnership that it forms with another individual is affected, but also its community, nation, and the global village. Your decision to evolve consciously through responsible choice contributes not only to your own evolution, but also to the evolution of all of those aspects of humanity in which you participate. It is not just you that is evolving through your decisions, but the entirety of humanity.

If you wish the world to become loving and compassionate, become loving and compassionate yourself. If you wish to diminish fear in the world, diminish your own. These are the gifts that you can give. The fear that exists between nations is a macrocosm of the fear that exists between individuals. The perception of power as external that separates nations is the same that exists between individuals; and the love, clarity, and compassion that emerge within the individual that chooses consciously to align itself with its soul is the same that will bring sexes, races, nations, and neighbors into harmony with each other. There is no other way.

Though each human being is responsible for the quality of Life that he or she personally experiences, simultaneously that extends into the macrocosm.

The threat of nuclear annihilation, for example, is a macrocosmic idea or notion on our Earth, and it requires the complete evolution of the microcosm in order for that to evaporate. So long as those who strive to establish harmony at the level of nations have within themselves the anger and violence that they seek to heal between nations, the harmony that they seek to create at the macrocosmic level cannot come into being. What is in one is in the whole, and therefore, ultimately, each soul is responsible for the whole world.

When you commit to a spiritual partnership with another human being, you bring the energy of the archetype of spiritual partnership into the physical arena. You begin to form and to live by the values, perceptions, and actions that reflect equality with your partner and a commitment to his or her spiritual development and your own. You begin to set aside the wants of your personality in order to accommodate the needs of your partner's spiritual growth, and, in doing that, you grow yourself. That is how spiritual partnership works.

You begin to see that what is necessary to the health of your partnership is identical with what is necessary to your own spiritual growth, that each of you holds the pieces that the other is missing. If you are jealous, for example, you will find that jealousy is what brings to the surface in your partner an aspect that needs to be healed, and that that aspect is mirrored in yourself. You begin to value your partner's contribution to your development. You experience that his or her perceptions and observations are helpful, and, indeed, central, to your growth, that conversations between you stir deep waters.

You learn the roles of love and commitment and trust in making your partnership work. You learn that love alone is not enough, that without trust, you are not able to give and to receive the love that both of you have for each other. You learn that your commitment must be translated into a form that satisfies the needs of both you and your partner. You learn to value the needs of your partner as much as you value your own, because the partnership that you both want requires two healthy and inwardly secure individuals.

You learn to trust not only each other, but also your ability to grow together. You learn that you put your partnership most at risk by avoiding that which you are most afraid will destroy it. It is not easy to express what is inside you, especially that which makes you feel vulnerable or painful or angry or upset. These are the emotions that empower words that can do either damage or can do so much healing. You learn that sharing your concerns with consideration and the intention to heal and trust in the process is the only appropriate avenue. As you approach your needs with courage instead of fear you ignite a sense of trust. The true human condition in its most perfect form has no secrets. It does not hide, but exists in clear love.

You learn not to do stupid and careless things to each other. You learn that wanting what you want is not enough, but that you must both want it deeply and create it every day, that you must bring it into being and hold it in being with your intentions. As the consciousness of each of you becomes lighter, your partnership becomes richer.

You learn the value of considering the other's position. By becoming the other person, by truly walking into the fears of the other and then returning into your own being again, you open up the conversation to transcend the personal and become healing at the impersonal. This allows you to see each other as spiritual playmates as you work through the areas that require healing in each of you. Even into the toughest moments of your work on feelings of insecurity you can be light and remind yourself that you are spirits who have taken on the physical experience and have far greater power than you are showing in that moment of weakness.

The things that are the individual's to learn in spiritual union with another individual are the group's, the community's, and the nation's to learn in spiritual union with other groups, communities, and nations. The choice in each instance is between learning through fear and doubt or through wisdom, between the lower-frequency energy currents of the personality and the higher-frequency energy currents of the soul. If the anger of one personality toward another creates distance, shatters intimacy, and causes defensiveness, the anger of one nation, or religion, or sex toward another produces the same. If the concern of one personality for another produces closeness, appreciation, and mutual regard, the concern of one nation, or religion, or community for another produces the same. The dynamic is identical.

You are related to every form of Life upon this planet and beyond. As your soul evolves, you move into greater awareness of the nature of that relationship, and the responsibilities that you assume.

Within our species there are degrees of soul consciousness. The significance of the evolution of responsibility is that each human being moves through levels of responsibility on its way to wholeness. In other words, as a soul chooses the lesson of responsibility, it will find itself incarnating into an atmosphere of more potential impact upon the species. The personality must also come to agree with what the soul has chosen. If you are not consciously ready, you will not be put into a position to impact many for the protection of your own soul.

A soul that is new to the human experience, for example, a soul that has evolved from the animal kingdom and is beginning its journey of human evolution, although there are very few of them at this point, begins within a certain frequency range, and for its own protection incarnates into a limited sphere of human life. It may incarnate into a remote region so that it can have a gentle life familiarizing itself with the human physical experience. As it becomes more adept at the human sensory system, at human intelligence, at the connection between the soul and body energy and what is expected within a human incarnation, its capacity to move and incarnate into more responsible centers of activity increases. Center of activity does not mean the presence of a city or a university, but an activity of karmic proportion.

In other words, a person that is living in a remote area in which the temptations of life and the definitions of good and evil are far more clear, and in which there are not as many temptations, is not in the same karmic center as a soul that has chosen to incarnate as one who would have a larger sphere of influence within a family, or a community, or a nation. A soul's center of activity refers to the degree of expansion of its karmic influence and energy influence. A soul needs to be more advanced to handle the possibilities that come from the expansion of its karmic energy influences. This is the significance of the evolution of responsibility.

As souls choose to participate consciously in more inclusive levels of interaction, they take on not only their own transformation, but also those of the larger collectives in which they participate. Think of your consciousness in terms of physical light. That light shines, but a brighter light shines over a wider range, and a dimmer light shines on a smaller range. The extent to which your light shines is the width and depth and breadth of your karmic influence. If you are a major light you shine upon the entire globe. If you are growing into a major light but are a lesser light you shine within a different range of which you are held karmically responsible, but your potential to shift your own quality of consciousness and the quality of consciousness of others is equally enormous.

Within the sphere of possibilities and probabilities for the soul there exist many opportunities, including the possibility that the soul might choose, for example, its most remote path of growth instead of the one that is most natural to its energy, so to speak. If, in the privacy of his or her own spiritual choices, as he or she advances in faith and in courage and in feelings for his or her own humanity, a soul may well open that door which leads to greater awareness and to greater karmic influence and responsibility. Whereas that possibility might have existed with only a small probability at the time of the soul's incarnation, a door that would open only under certain circumstances—if this happened and then if that happened—it may become so that the soul does indeed find its way to that path.

Every microconsciousness, or individual soul, affects the macroconsciousness depending upon its quality of Light, upon the frequency of its consciousness. A soul that agrees to incarnate into a lifetime in which it has significant potential to affect the lives of many is a great soul. The quality of power of such a soul is great. It is global. Its capacity to touch the lives of millions, and, indeed, billions of human beings is very real, and so will be its karmic debt if it fails in its task to advance humanity. It will have the karmic responsibility of billions of souls upon its own.

Great souls upon our planet, like all souls upon our planet, must make decisions moment by moment. As you look upon the many souls of our Earth who stand in major positions to maneuver the lives of thousands, or millions, or billions of human beings, allow yourself to distinguish them from their personalities. Even though a soul has the ability to influence the lives of billions of people, or even the entirety of humanity, its personality is tempted.

When the personality, Jesus, encountered the Luciferic principle, the challenging principle of our species, when he was offered dominion over the entire globe, the fulfillment of all that he could conceive, was he tempted? Yes, he was tempted. If he were not, there would have been no power in his choice. Were the choice of the path of glory that he chose not balanced against another of equal attraction, how could he have drawn such power from that choice? Authentic empowerment is not gained by making choices that do not stretch you.

When a soul chooses the vertical path, when it chooses to evolve consciously through responsible choice, it becomes capable of liberating itself from its own negativities. It reaches for authentic power. It takes on, so to speak, its own negativity, the unconscious intentions of the splintered parts of its personality. As a personality becomes conscious, as it evolves into a multisensory personality and becomes integrated, the frequency of its consciousness increases. It becomes whole. Its negativities drop away and the quality of its consciousness becomes lighter. It becomes able to see itself and those around it with compassion and clarity, with the wisdom of its soul.

When a soul chooses to participate consciously in more inclusive levels of interaction, it becomes capable of participating directly in the liberation of its family, or its group, or its community, or its nation from the negativities that are present and active at those levels. It also runs the risk of contamination by those negativities. In other words, a soul that seeks to bring a higher quality of consciousness to a more inclusive level of human interaction runs the risk of being contaminated by the fear, or the anger, or the selfishness of that level.

Great souls, such as the soul that was Gandhi, for example, run the risk of great contamination. At the level of soul contact, a great soul deals not only with its own fear, its personal fear, but it also takes on the evolution of the collective fear of the species. The weight of that is where a great soul risks contamination on a great level, but its possibility of releasing the fear from the collective consciousness of the species becomes also possible.

The consciousness of a great soul is symbolic of the larger consciousness, the macroconsciousness, that holds the same values and fears and guilts. That macroconsciousness might be the collective consciousness of the United States, or Russia, or Ethiopia. The many souls that form that collective are in continual dialogue with its own. The great soul is the person who has taken on the task of change. If he or she is able to transcend fear, to act out of courage, the whole of its group will benefit and each one, in his or her own life, will be suddenly more courageous, though they may not see how or why.

Not all souls accomplish the tasks that they have set for themselves. As you look at the individuals who are in major positions of influence upon our planet you can see whether or not they are succeeding in their tasks of advancing humanity by the choices that they have made. Some have chosen to align themselves, like mannequins, with the dying consciousness of the five-sensory human that has existed within the collective consciousness of each of our nations. They have chosen, in other words, to represent a system that is disintegrating, and so their own systems are disintegrating before their eyes. Their comrades are corrupt. Their governments are corrupt.

These souls represent a form of power that is no longer effective, but they have failed to understand that. They draw to themselves those whose consciousnesses are aligned symbolically and in terms of beliefs to their own. They choose to walk the shifting pattern of fear and selfishness. They exhibit great paranoiac energy, and, therefore, they attract to themselves, their governments, and their militaries fellow human beings that have the same paranoiac desire to destroy life, as if the destruction of life will save our planet, but it will not.

Through the decisions that they have made, these souls have refused to acknowledge that the older forms of power, the perception of power as external, no longer will be tolerated upon the Earth. Nonetheless, the evolution from external power to authentic power is occurring now in full force, and so their decisions affect only how that shift will take place. They have chosen the path of fear and doubt, of trauma and pain.

The difference between a great soul that aligns itself with

openness and growth and interdependence, that transcends its fear on behalf of itself and its collective, and one that does not is that the soul that chooses openness has a different active level of courage and insight and wisdom, and the one that does not has consistently weakened under the impact of the fear of the collective. Choice to choice to choice to choice, negativity upon negativity, and a Hitler is created. The soul that was Hitler had great potential as well.

Every soul that agrees consciously to bring to a level of human interaction the love and compassion and wisdom that it has acquired is trying through his or her own energy to challenge the fear patterns of that collective. This is the archetypical pattern that was put into place within our species by the Teacher, Jesus. It is what He symbolized as He moved through His lifetime in the way that He did. He released the negative karmic patterns of the collective unconscious that had accumulated to His time. In each great soul it is the same pattern—the pattern of taking on the whole through the power of his or her own consciousness to transform it.

When a soul reaches for authentic power and chooses consciously to bring that power into the levels of interaction that it shares with other souls, it enters this dynamic. It brings to a collective energy system the consciousness of authentic power, and through that power engages in the transformation of that collective.

Your evolution toward authentic power, therefore, affects not only you. As the frequency of your consciousness increases, as the quality of your consciousness reflects the clarity, humbleness, forgiveness, and love of authentic power, it touches more and more around you. As your temptations become greater, so does your ability to make responsible choices. As you shine brighter, as your Light and power increase with each responsible choice, so does your world.*

---

* To learn how to apply what you have learned in this chapter and deepen your experiences, see the Chapter 11 Study Guide on page 300.

— 12 —

Souls

Each human being has a soul. The journey toward individual soulhood is what distinguishes the human kingdom from the animal kingdom, the vegetable kingdom, and the mineral kingdom. Only the human kingdom has the experience of individual soulhood. That is why its powers of creation are great.

The soul process moves through degrees of awareness. Animals, for example, do not have individual souls. They have group souls. Each animal is a part of a group soul. Each horse is a part of the group soul of horse, each cat is a part of the group soul of cat, and so on. A group soul is not the same as an individual soul.

Consider, for example, the group soul of buffalo. There is

one group soul of enormous impersonal energy that is called "buffalo." It is an enormous expansive sphere of impersonal energy that is buffalo consciousness. It exists at a level of simply energy dynamics, not individual selfhood. That energy is in continual movement. As it heightens in frequency, it can spill over into the next level, and it also can absorb other frequencies from a lower level, so the soul continues. It is a group soul, not individual. There are not individual buffalo souls within a whole. There is only one soul energy system wherein there is no individualhood. Instinctual behavior is the way of the group soul.

Picture a movement that looks like the mouth of the Mississippi River. As you walk up the river from that place, the river grows more and more and more narrow until it reaches but a point of power. The open mouth area is analogous to a group soul. The size of it, the collective nature of it, is the group soul. This is the nature of the souls in the mineral, vegetable, and animal kingdoms. In other words, "cat" is a cat soul, "dolphin" is a dolphin soul, and so on.

Within the animal kingdom, there are graduations of intelligence and awareness. For example, dolphin, horse, and dog are not on the same wavelength. The consciousness of the dolphin is closer to the consciousness of the ape, and then closer to the consciousness of the dog, but the consciousness of the horse is on a level beneath them. It is possible that the human soul can be produced through the evolution of the animal kingdom as a collective energy from the animal soul.

How does this happen?

The dolphin soul, for example, evolves through each particular individual dolphin. The particular advancements of each particular dolphin advance the soul of the dolphin itself. The collective is enhanced by the accomplishments of the individual dolphin. The same mechanism works within the human kingdom. With each of our individual advancements, the group soul of humanity—what we call our collective unconscious—evolves. In this way, evolution continues within the dolphin species, as within all species.

Let us say, arbitrarily, that the consciousness of the dog soul is twenty percentile points below that of the dolphin soul, twenty points less than the intelligence of the dolphin. If the group soul of dog produces high Light consciousness, it is possible for that consciousness to release itself from the group soul of dog and advance into and penetrate the consciousness of dolphin. Likewise, it is possible, and it does happen, that human beings' souls come from the advanced soul energy of the dolphin soul or the ape soul, and begin their process of evolution into the human soul.

Unlike an animal, you have an individual soul. You are an individual energy system, a micro of a macro. As part of the micro, you have all the power of the macro calibrated to an individual form of certain energies. Animals are not micros of a macro. Cats, for example, do not have individual souls or ego energy. They are merely physical manifestations of a huge macro system. That certain cats are scared and certain are comforted is merely the different numerous millions of frequencies that interact into the group cat soul.

Animals do not evolve through responsible choice as we

do. Rather, the frequency of their consciousnesses becomes Lightened in the fullness of the evolution of their soul as a group. This does not mean that animals are not capable of individual acts of love. What of an animal that lays down its life for its human? That is as legitimate a sacrifice of love of life as it is for a human, because in that instance the animal realizes that it is willingly releasing its life. That, for an animal, is graduation to the human experience, or to its next higher level.

The nature of a group soul can be seen through its manifestations. The nature of dolphin soul, for example, is expressed through dolphins. The same is true for our species. The nature of the soul of humankind can be seen through the nature of human beings.

The dolphin soul is leaving the Earth, that is, the dolphin species is becoming extinct. The dolphins are beaching themselves. They are creating diseases within themselves. This is their way of refusing to continue to live upon the Earth. They feel that they cannot fulfill the purpose for which they are born. Therefore, they are leaving. Their deaths are not suicides because they are not frightened. They are exhausted.

The dolphin soul manifests itself—dolphins are born—to bring love and life and creativity to the oceans. They manifest to form a bridge of joy and love and intelligence between the aquatic kingdom and the human kingdom. This they cannot do. Our species reaches toward the dolphin soul only with brutality.

The dolphin spirit—how it suffers! This is a time of great

sorrow. It is a time to look soberly and deeply upon the values and behaviors that result from the perception of power as external. It is a time to grieve with the dolphin soul, to offer comfort to it.

If you wish to offer comfort to the dolphin soul, image from the heart of the dolphin consciousness that your energies are moving below deep warm clear soothing water. As you feel yourself emerging into the aquatic kingdom, let yourself begin to radiate your thoughts to these fellow creatures that share our planetary home. Image that you are sending them love as they continue their evolution and leave the Earth school, that you grieve with them and yet you know that, like you, they are immortal. Send these thoughts. Let them know they are not leaving without human beings' understanding. Let them hear you say, "I am one who understands."

Can you do that?

It will make their grieving journey of value.

There is more than one avenue from which individual souls are formed. Part of the chain of evolution within our global village is the process of this advancement from kingdom to kingdom to kingdom, but if a soul that has not been before upon our planet chooses the human experience, it would not be necessary for that soul to move through kingdom evolution. It would, indeed, pick up the situation within the physical environment that is most appropriate for it.

There are souls that have never had the human experience. When we speak of souls entering the physical arena to heal, to balance their energy, to pay their karmic debts, we are speaking of the evolution of Life as we know it upon our Earth. We are not speaking of other galaxies, or of Life on other levels that are not physical as we know them. The experience of physicalness is not always necessary to certain advances. If it is, it is encouraged.

There comes a point when the physicalness experience no longer serves the soul's awareness, and, therefore, the soul chooses to learn in the nonphysical realm. It may choose to learn, for example, through the task of becoming a non-physical guide. Each individual human soul is a micro of the macro that is the soul of the human species, but the soul of humankind is not a micro of a macro. In other words, there is no larger spiritual human soul beyond the soul of humanity. Beyond that comes the experience of master, the experience of moving into advanced levels of Light that is no longer specific to human.

Our nonphysical Teachers are from these levels of Light. Therefore, it is not appropriate to consider them from the dynamic of the personal. Rather, it is more appropriate to think of them as impersonal consciousnesses, which is that which they are, from realms that cannot be understood in human terms. They do not, for example, have the splintered personality aspects that we have. They do not have shadow sides, so to speak. Does an Angel have a soul? An Angel is its soul, its full soul.

That is the difference between that which is whole and in

union and that which is growing into it. Duality only exists in certain levels, and not in others. Duality is a dynamic of learning. It is its own rhythm and tension and does not exist beyond another level of learning and development. You are existing in duality, and your nonphysical Teachers are not.

This is not their home, so to speak. They are teachers to our plane. They are free to teach in our plane without being of our plane. Your nonphysical Teacher does not become of this plane when it counsels you any more than a parent becomes an infant in order to teach its infant. It is not necessary. That level of evolution is assumed in the presence of the parent. It is simply the natural dynamic of evolution.

We are destined to evolve beyond the nature of duality. Duality is that which is understood in time and space. As you evolve beyond that, and also when you leave your physical body and journey home to your nonphysical plane of reality, you will not exist in dualism, and that sense of the wrathful, or sorrowful, or fearful self that you think of as present to you now will evaporate. It has no power in the realm beyond duality where there exists the perfection of all that is. When you leave your physical form, you will join the nonphysical level of reality that is appropriate to your vibrational frequency at the time that you leave your incarnation.

Where do advanced human souls go?

There are many forms of Life that exist as advancements of this one. There are literally millions of options. There is life in numerous galaxies. There are millions, indeed, billions of other life-filled planets. There is not one planet that lacks a level of active consciousness, some of which is akin to our human form, and some of which does not come close to our form, but remains consciousness as we understand the term.

There exists a realm that the religious language of the West would call the Angelic kingdom. This is a range of beings of numerous frequencies and qualities of consciousness, many of whom guide and interact with us upon the Earth. This realm is indeed balanced with other forces, but it cannot be understood in human terms. Evolution continues in that realm, although there is that perception that our words "harmony" and "perfectness" would address. An Angel might be thought of as a force of consciousness that has evolved into an appropriate teaching modality for the planetary village called Earth, but may also have been a part of the evolution of other galaxies and Life forms there.

An Angel's home, so to speak, is that kingdom, the Angelic kingdom, and the range of nonphysical Life forms that exist within and lower than and beyond that vibrational sphere. Angels continue evolution, as do other members of that realm, as do those consciousnesses that we would recognize as masters, such as those after whom religions have been named upon our Earth. That evolution continues, but there is perfectness rather than the experience of fusing consciousness with matter that occurs within our Earth school.

Does the law of karma apply to nonphysical beings?

The law of karma is universal in the sense that there is not a Life form that is not responsible for its energy, but karma cannot be understood in terms of nonphysical dimensions in the same way that we understand it. An Angel does not have the barriers that we have. An Angel sees something, for example, and we do not. The difference is a barrier. An Angel does not have our barriers, and so it cannot create the karma that we do. It has a level of sight and knowledge that prevents certain actions from happening simply because of the depth of knowingness that is of its rank in creation.

The great law of karma works because an Angel still has will, but an Angel is armed with a great deal more than the limitation that characterizes the human experience. An Angel does not fear death. It has no physicalness. It is only that it is immortal. It is with all that is. It has no doubt. It sees and lives in Light, so the ingredients that create karma for the human experience are not part of its personal reality. Although an Angel has will, the circumstances cannot be described in which that will might bend in the wrong way, if there were such a thing, or in a negative way. In one sense, an Angel can be considered to have evolved beyond the need to be tested, and, therefore, for it, there is no karma.

Other levels also exist, such as the level in which disincarnate spirits are bound close to their physicalness in the immediate environment of the Earth arena. These spirits do not pursue the journey back to their higher selves, but remain bound with their nonphysical individual states close to the Earth.

Imagine that your personality, your characteristics, and part of your nonphysical self wish to remain intact and not proceed on their evolution. The process of the soul discharging the aspects of personality does not happen. A combustion and congestion occurs within the energy system. Usually this happens when a soul cannot accept that it must move on and release a particular incarnation. In some instances, a soul holds on to a personality because that personality was particularly successful or powerful in its lifetime.

The congestion in the process of evolution that occurs produces the phenomena that we refer to as evil spirits, ghosts, or possessions. These spirits choose to remain Earthbound, within the Earth's auric field. Are they evil? They are negative, yes, but evil is another issue. Do they encourage negativity? Yes, but that is part of the law of attraction; their own energy is drawn to like forces of energy, or like forces of weakness. Within this realm, these spirits can create additional negative karma by pursuing malevolence.

Therefore, it is possible to speak of evolving beyond karma, as the Buddhas do. They are referring to the karma of the Earth, where there is always this circumstance of choice between how you want to learn, which path shall you choose. The Buddhas refer to the Earth, to the human experience and how it is set up, which is with free will, choice, placed between faith and doubt, good and evil, between the choices and dualisms that our species has created. It is that karma that they are referring to, not the karmic patterns that cease to be once you, as a soul, no longer require learning in the world of duality. Even though Angels have will they do not accumulate karma as we think of it. It is not part of their dimension. Yet they have will. The law of karma as we understand it is the law of karma for physical matter and spirit, not for spirit.

Many realms that are nonphysical are not Angelic. In addition to the realm of disincarnate human beings that are bound close to the Earth, for example, there is the Devic community of our Nature kingdoms. There are numerous, numerous realms of nonphysical life. Beyond the Angelic realm are realms upon realms of intelligence that we would think of as God.

Within the human species there exist degrees of soul consciousness. Not all humans are equally aware of their souls. Therefore, do all human beings have equal potential?

Yes and no. This question is complex. It cannot be answered simply because among souls that are on the same frequency band, such as those within the Earth school, there is a common quality of consciousness, yet there is a difference between their ranges of consciousness. An individual that is not quite as expanded in his or her awareness is not equal in the sense that we usually mean equal to someone of greater awareness. There is an inequality. Yet it is not an inequality that remains unequal. It is just a temporary level of momentum in the flow of evolution.

A soul has no beginning and no end, and yet some souls are older than other souls. Both are true. All souls come directly from the Godhead, and yet there is no single way that souls are formed individually. Both are true. Understanding the soul becomes paradoxical only if you apply a type of thinking that holds the notion of beginning.

All that is can form itself into individual droplets of consciousness. Because you are part of All that is, you have literally always been, yet there was the instant when that individual energy current that is you was formed. Consider that the ocean is God. It has always been. Now reach in and grab a cup full of water. In that instant, the cup becomes individual, but it has always been, has it not? This is the case with your soul. There was the instant when you became a cup of energy, but it was of an immortal original Being.

You have always been because what it is that you are is God, or Divine Intelligence, but God takes on individual forms, droplets, reducing its power to small particles of individual consciousness. It is a massive reduction of power, yet the power is as full in that droplet as it is in the whole. It is as immortal and as creative and as expressive but in its tinier form its energy is reduced appropriately to its form. As that little form grows in power, in selfhood, in its own consciousness of self, it becomes larger and more Godlike. Then it becomes God.

This is a process that parallels the process of your personality, which is of your soul, expanding into your higher self, and thereby coming into the full power of your soul incarnate. It also parallels the process of your personality and higher self reentering the fullness of your soul when you leave the Earth. As an individual soul, you remain an individual soul. You are both individual and one with All that is.

The individual unit of evolution is the soul. This perception is new to us because, as a species, we have not before been aware of the existence of the soul. In our religious thoughts we acknowledge what we call the soul, but we have not, until now, taken it seriously enough to consider what the existence of the soul means in terms of everyday experience, in terms of the joys and pains and sorrows and fulfillments that make a human life.

We have not turned our attention to the needs of the soul. We have not considered what is required by the soul in order to be healthy. We have not studied the soul, or sought to help it attain what is necessary to its evolution and its health. Because we have been five-sensory, we have focused upon the body and the personality. We have developed an extensive knowledge of the physical apparatus that the soul assumes when it incarnates. We know of amino acids, neurotransmitters, chromosomes, and enzymes, but we do not know of the soul. We do not know how these physical functions serve the soul, or are affected by it.

We seek to cure dysfunctions of the body by controlling its environment at the molecular level. In other words, our approach to healing is based upon the perception of power as external. This type of healing can be helpful to the body, but it does not, and cannot, heal at the level of the soul.

Consider that those who are trained in this way are accustomed to learning about Life through the study of dead matter. They seek to learn of Life through the study of carcasses and corpses. Through the study of that which does not have spirit, how can they see spirit? Even as such minds look out into this vast galaxy, they cannot see Life because they are convinced that the entire galaxy does not have Life, except as they see it and identify it, so the Life forms and the brothers and sisters that we have on other galaxies remain hidden, and will remain hidden until the basic premise that Life is and permeates all that is, that there is only Life, becomes the principle of what we call science. Then we will explore the physics of the soul. Then we will study Life with Life and not dead matter and not try to breathe intelligence and purpose into it by taking apart in our laboratories human forms and animal forms. This will be seen someday as a very primitive form of learning because there is no consciousness there.

The body is the instrument of the soul. If the piano player is sick, does it help to repair his or her piano? What an instrument produces depends not only upon the state of the instrument, but also upon the musician. If the musician plays the blues, or soars with joy, the instrument follows. Even a tuned and polished instrument cannot soar with joy if the musician chooses sadness or grief. In the case of your soul and body, the instrument becomes the blues, or soars with joy. If the musician becomes consumed with grief, or anger, or sadness, the instrument disintegrates. In some cases, a broken instrument can be repaired, but a repair at that level cannot cure what caused the breakdown.

After several years of marriage to a willful partner, an acquaintance of mine found herself suffocating in the relationship, unable to express her deepest desires and her creativity. One winter morning her husband's Jeep, which was parked on their steep driveway, broke loose and rolled over her, crushing her pelvic area. Surgery and chemicals healed her hips and eased the pain of her body, but can surgery mend the damage that is done when a woman's creativity—represented, in this case, by her pelvic area, her reproductive capability, the physical symbol of her feminine creativity—is crushed by the uncontrolled macho masculinity of her husband—represented, in this case, by a runaway Jeep? Can chemicals ease the pain of a suffering soul?

Is it chance that one person develops heart disease, while another develops cancer? Even though disease states have correlations to factors of diet, exercise, lifestyle, and heredity, these correlations cannot mask the fact that life, for some people, is a heartbreak, while others allow themselves to be consumed, to be eaten alive, by the negative experiences of their lives. Can bypass surgery or chemotherapy heal that?

Are the numerous ways that physical dysfunctions occur without meaning? Health for some people is a matter of the heart, for others a matter of what they can digest or eliminate in the course of their lives, for others a matter of the head, and for others a matter of being able to hear, or to see, or to move through their lives flexibly, or to stand on their own, or literally to handle the experiences of their lives. These are the issues that must be addressed directly and openly and honestly in the creation of health.

This does not mean that it is inappropriate to care for the body, or to see a physician in times of illness. Even though the physical is not as real, so to speak, as the nonphysical, it is, nonetheless, the lowest, densest projection of spiritual matter, and, therefore, it must be honored. It must be honored. The body needs rest, and it needs care, but behind every aspect of the health or illness of the body is the energy of the soul.

It is the health of the soul that is the true purpose of the human experience.

Everything serves that.*

---

* To learn how to apply what you have learned in this chapter and deepen your experiences, see the Chapter 12 Study Guide on page 306.

POWER

— 13 —

Psychology

Psychology means soul knowledge. It means the study of the spirit, but it has never been that. Psychology is the study of cognitions, perceptions, and affects. It is the study of the personality.

Because psychology is based upon the perceptions of the five-sensory personality, it is not able to recognize the soul. It is not able to understand the dynamics that underlie the values and behaviors of the personality. Just as medicine seeks to heal the body without recognizing the energy of the soul that lies behind the health or illness of the body, and, therefore, cannot heal the soul, psychology seeks to heal the personality without recognizing the force of the soul that lies behind the configuration and experiences of the personality, and, therefore, also cannot heal at the level of the soul.

In order to develop and nurture your mind and your body, it is necessary to realize that you have a mind and a body. To heal directly at the level of the soul it is first necessary to acknowledge that you *have* a soul. If you have a soul, is it a hollowness that mythologically fills your rib cage? No. If, then, your soul is real and alive with force and beingness, what is its purpose?

To develop a healthy and disciplined mind, an intellect that can expand wholesomely and fully into any task, requires more than merely recognizing the existence of the mind. It requires understanding how the mind works, what it desires, what strengthens it and what weakens it, and then applying that knowledge. In the same way, it is not possible to consciously assist the soul in its evolution merely by recognizing the existence of the soul. It is necessary to understand the soul's temperament, to learn what the soul can tolerate and what it cannot tolerate, what contributes to its health and what breaks its health down. These things must be looked at.

The means for doing this have not yet been developed. We have not yet created a disciplined and systematic understanding of the soul. We do not understand how our behaviors and activities affect the soul. When we see the personality in dysfunction, we do not think of what this reveals about the soul. Yet the personality is specific aspects of the soul reduced to a physical form. Therefore, dysfunctions of the personality cannot be understood without an understanding of the soul.

The fears, angers, and jealousies that deform the personality cannot be understood apart from the karmic circumstances that they serve. When you understand, and truly understand, that the experiences of your life are necessary to the balancing of the energy of your soul, you are free to not react to them personally, to not create more negative karma for your soul.

Pain by itself is merely pain, but the experience of pain coupled with an understanding that the pain serves a worthy purpose is suffering. Suffering is meaningful. Suffering can be endured because there is a reason for it that is worth the effort. What is more worthy of your pain than the evolution of your soul?

This does not mean that you become a martyr. When you understand that by consciously serving the evolution of your soul you contribute the most that you can to your world, you become one who contributes consciously to the well-being and spiritual development of those who share the human learning experience with you. If you are unkind to yourself you will be unkind to others, and if you are negligent of yourself you will be that to others. Only by feeling compassion for yourself can you feel compassion for others.

If you cannot love yourself, you cannot love others and you cannot stand to see others loved. If you cannot treat your own self kindly you will resent that treatment when you see it in anyone else. If you cannot love yourself, loving others becomes a very painful endeavor with only occasional moments of comfort. In other words, loving others, or how you treat yourself, is your own dose of your own medicine that you really give to others at the same time.

Individuals who experience what might be thought of as a martyr attitude see themselves as giving all that they have to others. They see this as a form of loving, but in truth the love that they give is contaminated because it is so filled with sorrow for themselves. A sense of guilt and powerlessness clouds the energy from their hearts and so when their affection is felt by another it does not feel good, actually. It feels somehow thick with need, yet the need is never articulated, so their love feels like cement pulling you.

When you can do kindly things to yourself then you know what it is to be able to love yourself. Then you can look at others who desperately need kindness and love and feel good about their getting it, not patronizing, but truly good. This is the energy of the soul. This is the perception of the soul. When there is no compassion, when there is guilt, remorse, anger, or sorrow, there is opportunity to heal the soul. What is the relationship of these experiences to a healthy soul and to a soul that is not healthy? What is a healthy soul?

A spiritual psychology is necessary to answer these questions, a new discipline of the spirit that is truly of the spirit, that has as its focus the soul of the human being. Human evolution, and the evolution of the spirit in matter, is a very specific evolution. It is not haphazard. It is not chaotic. It is very specific. When certain necessary processes of the maturation of the union of matter and spirit are not honored, the spirit breaks down. Psychologists have attempted to explain these breakdowns in the terms of psychology. We can continue to use that language, but let psychology then expand to include a language of the spirit. This will eventually become its first tongue, so to speak, and all psychoses and psychotic breakdown will finally, eventually, be put into its proper language, which is shattered spirit.

Reincarnation and the role of karma in the development of the soul will be central parts of spiritual psychology. The characteristics of a personality, the qualities that make one personality different from another, cannot be appreciated without an understanding of the karma that created those characteristics. They cannot always be understood in terms of the history of the personality because they may reflect experiences that predate the personality, in some cases by centuries. At issue, therefore, is not the effects of anger, jealousy, bitterness, sorrow, and so forth upon the personality, but upon the soul.

An understanding of each of the personalities, each of the lifetimes, of a soul is not necessary. The numerous, numerous lifetimes of a soul are not equally central to the development of each of its personalities, but without awareness of the experiences of those lifetimes that bear directly upon the struggles of your personality, you cannot understand the extent of what is being healed through your experiences, or seeking to come to conclusion. If your soul was a Roman centurion, an Indian beggar, a Mexican mother, a nomad boy, and a medieval nun, among other incarnations, for example, and if the karmic patterns that were set into motion within those lifetimes are in motion within you, you will not be able to understand your proclivities, or interests, or ways of responding to different situations without an awareness of the experiences of those lifetimes.

It may be that the medieval nun of your soul developed an ability to see an Angel. What an extraordinary spiritual achievement! Your nonphysical Teacher will come to you upon those same frequencies of Light. She gives to you the fruits of a lifetime of contemplation and struggle and pain and courage. The Roman centurion of your soul is not dead millennia ago. That energy can literally step into your body and want to hold a modern weapon out of curiosity.

Do you dislike certain types of people? Were you drawn to medicine as a child? Are you frightened of small places? Reactions such as these are not always explainable in terms of the experiences of your life. The healing power at the core of psychology is the power of consciousness. Seeking out, facing with courage, and bringing into the Light of consciousness that which is unconsciousness, and, therefore, in a position of power over the personality, is what heals. When that which needs to be made conscious is not recognized to exist—such as the experiences of lifetimes that were lived in other places and at other times—it cannot be healed in this way.

Have you left a partner or a spouse? Has a spouse or a partner left you? It may be that your souls have graciously and with great compassion agreed to enact within this lifetime a situation that they have experienced together in another lifetime, or other lifetimes, a situation that still has healing potential for both. It may be that your souls have agreed to a mutual balancing of energy, so that one experiences the same painful loss that it inflicted previously upon the other. Experiences such as these are not meant to cause meaningless pain. There is not one act in the Universe that is not compassionate.

Your parents are the souls to whom you are closest in your lifetime, and whose influence upon you is the greatest. This is so even if it does not appear that way, even if, for example, you were separated from your parents, or a parent, at birth. Your soul and the souls of your parents agreed to your relationship in order to balance the energy that each needed to balance, or to activate dynamics within each other that are essential to lessons that each must learn. Without an awareness of your karmic interactions, of the experiences of other lifetimes of your soul, you are not able to understand the depth of the potential awakenings that can result from your interactions with a parent, or a sibling.

The exploration and understanding of intuition will be a central part of spiritual psychology. Intuition is the voice of the nonphysical world. It is the communication system that releases the five-sensory personality from the limitations of its five-sensory system, that permits the multisensory personality to be multisensory. It is the connection between the personality and its higher self and its guides and Teachers.

Psychology does not even recognize the intuition, except

as a curiosity. Therefore, it does not recognize the knowledge that is obtained through the intuition, and, therefore, this knowledge is not processed by the intellect. The five-sensory personality processes only the knowledge that it gathers and substantiates through its five senses. The multisensory personality acquires knowledge through its intuition, and, in processing that knowledge, aligns itself, step by step, with its soul. The conscious path to authentic power requires recognition of the nonphysical dimensions of the human being, of the soul, and a growing knowledge of what the soul is and what it wants.

Spirituality will be at the core of spiritual psychology. Spiritual psychology will be oriented toward spirituality and spiritual crises will be considered legitimate sufferings. Spiritual psychology will trace and understand the functional relationships between karma, reincarnation, intuition, and spirituality.

Spirituality has to do with the immortal process itself. You have your intuition, for example, but your spirituality is not limited to your personality and its intuitional system. Your spirituality encompasses your whole soul's journey, whereas your intuition is the way that your soul can contact your beingness to help it in survival situations, or in creative situations, or in inspirational situations. It is the way that, through your higher self, you can ask and receive assistance from other souls and from your Teachers and guides. Your spirituality pertains to that which is immortal within you, whereas, when you leave your body, the intuitional system that was developed for that body will be left behind because it will no longer be necessary.

Spiritual psychology is a disciplined and systematic study of what is necessary to the health of the soul. It will identify behaviors that operate in opposition to harmony and wholeness, in opposition to the energy of the soul. It will consider the broad-reaching elements of negativity, and how many forms of negativity there are, and the effects of these upon the soul.

Anything that increases separation within a person shatters the soul or in some form diminishes its strength, not to be confused with its immortality. The soul, as it reduces itself to fit into a physical incarnation, has the blueprint of holism in it. A genetic spiritual pattern, so to speak, of holism is there and present, and when the personality operates outside of the genetic pattern of holism, dysfunction results.

Spiritual psychology will bring to light those situations that would shatter the spirit if seen clearly. Brutality, for example, shatters the human spirit. The soul cannot tolerate brutality. It cannot tolerate abundances of pain and irrationality. It cannot tolerate being lied to. Consider *that* on our planet. It cannot tolerate non-forgiveness. It cannot tolerate jealousies and hatreds. These are contaminants, poisons, for it.

When the personality engages in these behaviors, it is as though it feeds its body arsenic again and again. It is just like that. These behaviors distort and contaminate and destroy the strength of the soul, in the same way. This is the distortedness of the soul that the physical reduced counterpart of the soul, called the personality, takes on in order to cleanse, in order to let other souls see so that it can be helped.

Understanding this dynamic is at the heart of spiritual psychology. It is the foundation upon which spiritual psychology is built so that when pain is seen it is not responded to with judgment or ugliness or avoidance, but recognized as the soul shattered. In this way, we shall say, in this circumstance, let us heal him. Let us heal her. Let us not run from the unattractiveness of a shattered soul.

The personality of a shattered soul is unaware. There is a continual interaction between your personality and your soul. The question is are you aware of it or are you not? If you are not aware of it, then it is not direct. It is indirect through having to move its currents through the density of doubt, through the density of unawareness. If you are aware of the guidance from your higher self, and are receptive to it, that receptivity allows guidance to flow instantly and immediately. If you are unaware and deny that there is any level of higher wisdom and guidance to your life, then the guidance must come through the density of physical events.

Awareness first enters into an unaware personality through crisis. When the personality is not attached to, or is apart from, clear soul energy, it becomes seduced into the physical matterness of life. That always results in a personality crisis because the necessary strength and guidance that are meant to flow into the personality have been cut off. The personality that is unaware of, or denies the existence of, its higher sources of wisdom cannot draw upon its guidance, its intuition, or any of the guiding mechanisms of our species. Therefore, crisis results.

Was it meant that crisis be central to our growth? No. This pattern evolved through the choices that were made by our species. The flow of our evolution did not have to include this pattern of crisis. It did not have to include the experiences of pain and trauma, of emotional or physical violence and brutality in order to grow. It was given in Divine order that our species would move into wholeness at some point in its evolution. How it moved and learned in the course of its evolution was left to be determined by the choices that our species made of how to maneuver energy within the Earth school. Doubt was created and chosen as the major teacher through human choice itself. Our species chose this way of learning, and, therefore, set karmic patterns into motion, generational karmic patterns.

As our species evolved, as it experienced its spectrum of fears, its spectrum of desires, its spectrum of attachments to the physical, collectively and individually certain choices began to characterize and form the path that would be most familiar to us. Awakening into the need to touch something more, to touch one's own spiritual energy system, is now a well-worn path that includes the experience of becoming physically powerless in relation to the structure of the Earth school before the soul will reach for genuine power.

In other words, the awakening of the personality to the potential of the soul has come to require the loss of a mate, or the death of a child, or the collapse of a business, or some situation that renders the individual powerless. It requires the failure of external power. That, to the five-sensory personality, is crisis.

Spiritual psychology addresses this situation by addressing directly the issue of authentic power. It is timely because it comes at a time when our species is evolving beyond the five-sensory personality, beyond learning through five-sensory exploration of the physical world, which is external power, and into the experiences of the multisensory personality, the experiences of the nonphysical world and the conscious journey toward authentic power through responsible choice with the assistance of nonphysical guides and Teachers.

The personality, including the five-sensory personality, is neither positive nor negative. It is a tool of the soul, a natural part of incarnation. The development of the five senses was a celebration in which the intellect was expanded and our species was allowed to learn through physical matter. The quest for external power came to be generated by insecurity not because of the limitations of the five-sensory personality, but because of the choices that were made by our species to learn through fear and doubt instead of through wisdom.

Our species is again being given the chance to choose how it will learn, how it will evolve. This is a time for us as a species and as individuals to choose again. It is an opportunity for us as a species and as individuals to choose differently, to choose otherwise, to choose this time to learn love through wisdom, to take the vertical path of clarity, of conscious growth and conscious life.

We are coming to the end of a phase of evolution that was written long before we existed. When the learning and evolution of our species was designed, it was designed to complement cycles, great cycles that work within the Universe, within our galaxy and within others. These cycles move within physical form at certain speeds, serving certain purposes and balances of energies.

The cycle that we are ending, and, therefore, beginning, is of a moment in which three cycles come to conclusion and begin again. These cycles act one inside of the other. Just as the moon orbits the earth which orbits the sun and there are orbits within orbits, so, too, there are cycles within cycles. We are coming to the close of a grand cycle astrologically, a two thousand year cycle, and an even grander cycle, where a twenty-five thousand year cycle is linking with a conclusion of a one hundred and twenty-five thousand year cycle. That is why these things, within this moment in our evolution, are happening now. This is when they were meant to be.

The negativity of the last two thousand year cycle is being collected now so that it can be discharged and transformed, so that the next cycle of two thousand years which starts with the next beginning cycle of twenty-five thousand years and the next beginning cycle of one hundred twenty-five thousand years, all three simultaneously, can begin fresh.

This is what this present situation and moment upon our Earth is about: the birth of very different opportunities, opportunities to release patterns that are no longer necessary. The more Light, literally, the more en-Lightened that you are, the more you will choose different ways.

Spiritual psychology will support the choice to learn through wisdom, the choice to release patterns of negativity, of doubt and fear, that are no longer appropriate to who we are and what we are becoming. It will make clear the relationship between the personality and the soul, the differences between them, and how to recognize those differences. It will make explicit the effects of interactions between personalities from the perspective of the impersonal energy dynamics that they set into motion, and it will show how these dynamics can be used to heal.*

---

* To learn how to apply what you have learned in this chapter and deepen your experiences, see the Chapter 13 Study Guide on page 312.

14

Illusion

Each interaction with each individual is part of a continual learning dynamic. When you interact with another, an illusion is part of this dynamic. This illusion allows each soul to perceive what it needs to understand in order to heal. It creates, like a living picture show, the situations that are necessary to bring into wholeness the aspects of each soul that require healing.

The illusion is a learning vehicle. It is of the personality. You will leave the illusion behind when you die, when you return home. Yet a personality that lives in love and Light, that sees through the eyes of its soul, metaphorically speaking, can see the illusion and simultaneously not be drawn into it. This is an authentically empowered personality.

The illusion is exquisitely intimate to the needs of each soul. Always each situation serves each person involved. You cannot, and will not, encounter a circumstance, or a single moment, that does not serve directly and immediately the need of your soul to heal, to come into wholeness. The illusion for each soul is created by its intentions. Therefore, the illusion is alive at each moment with the most appropriate experiences that you can have in order for your soul to heal.

The illusion is malleable. This does not mean that what is created jointly within the illusion does not have an independence of the individual souls that participated in its creation. It means that there is no perception that cannot be healed, just as there is no intention that cannot be changed, or replaced with another. Understanding how the illusion comes into being, how it works, the dynamics behind it, and the role that it plays in the evolution of the soul is at the heart of spiritual psychology.

Spiritual psychology allows the personality to detach itself from the illusion and, therefore, to see it from a knowledgeable perspective, to see it in action. Just as, for example, an intelligence with a knowledge of modern medicine would be able to live among the populations of Europe during the time of the bubonic plague and not be affected by it, a personality with knowledge of the illusion and how it works is able to live within it and not be affected by it.

Bubonic plague is transmitted by fleas on rodents. This is known now but it was not known then. By keeping his or her environment clean, by avoiding all that attracts rodents, and by practicing personal hygiene, such a person could not only survive, but also keep others safe as well. When we experience fear or anger or jealousy, we are in an illusion that is designed to bring to awareness those parts of the soul that require healing. These things do not actually exist. That is why pursuing them does not bring power. What exists between souls is love, and that is all that exists. By understanding this, the personality is able to remain aware within the illusion, to accept consciously the healing that it offers, and to help others heal as well. The power of awareness and knowledge is identical in both situations.

The illusion holds power over you when you are not able to remember that you are a powerful spirit that has taken on the physical experience for the purpose of learning. It has power over you when you are compelled by the wants and impulses and values of your personality. It holds power over you when you fear and hate and sorrow and fester in anger or strike out in rage. It has no power over you when you love, when compassion opens your heart to others, when your creativity flows unimpeded joyously into the present moment. In other words, the illusion has no power over a personality that is fully aligned with its soul.

The illusion is governed by impersonal energy dynamics. It is shaped initially by the law of karma. The configuration of each personality, the unconscious intentions with which it is born, is determined by the karma of its soul. These intentions shape that personality's illusion, its reality within the Earth school, until they are replaced by other intentions, unconscious or conscious. If the reactions of the personality create additional karma for the soul, and if that karma cannot be balanced within the lifetime of the personality, that karma contributes to the shaping of another personality, and the intentions of that personality create its illusion, its reality within the Earth school, and so on.

Even after a personality becomes conscious and aware of its illusion, and sets its intentions accordingly, the karmic obligations of its soul must still be met. Karma is karma. Energy is energy. The awakened personality understands this, and therefore, does not respond to the experiences and the events of its life with anger, fear, sorrow, or jealousy, which would create additional negative karma for its soul, but with compassion and with trust that the Universe, in each moment, is attending to the needs of its soul. This draws to it other souls with the same frequency of consciousness.

Each personality draws to itself personalities with consciousness of like frequency, or like weakness. The frequency of anger attracts the frequency of anger, the frequency of greed attracts greed, and so on. This is the law of attraction. Negativity attracts negativity, just as love attracts love. Therefore, the world of an angry person is filled with angry people, the world of a greedy person is filled with greedy people, and a loving person lives in a world of loving people.

The law of attraction creates a cocoon, so to speak, of like energy around each personality so that as it seeks to heal its anger, or its fear, or its jealousy, the metamorphosis process into wholeness is intensified and accelerated, is brought

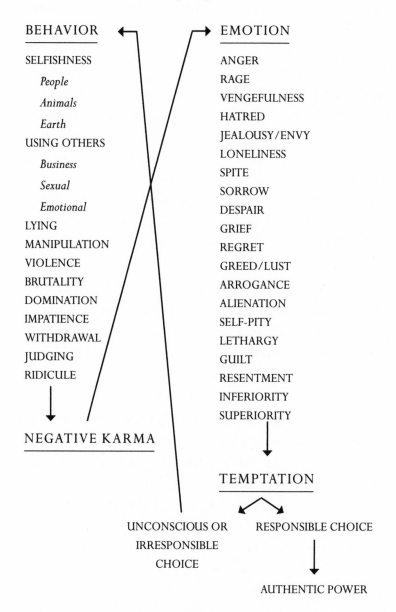

ILLUSION

POWERLESSNESS
(Fear)

BEHAVIOR	EMOTION

BEHAVIOR	EMOTION
SELFISHNESS	ANGER
People	RAGE
Animals	VENGEFULNESS
Earth	HATRED
USING OTHERS	JEALOUSY/ENVY
	LONELINESS
Business	SPITE
Sexual	SORROW
Emotional	DESPAIR
LYING	GRIEF
MANIPULATION	REGRET
VIOLENCE	GREED/LUST
BRUTALITY	ARROGANCE
DOMINATION	ALIENATION
IMPATIENCE	SELF-PITY
WITHDRAWAL	LETHARGY
JUDGING	GUILT
RIDICULE	RESENTMENT
	INFERIORITY
	SUPERIORITY

NEGATIVE KARMA

TEMPTATION

UNCONSCIOUS OR
IRRESPONSIBLE
CHOICE

RESPONSIBLE CHOICE

AUTHENTIC POWER

to the center of the stage of awareness. The personality sees its anger or its fear not only within itself, but everywhere outside itself as well. If the personality chooses consciously to heal its anger, or its fear, every circumstance, every encounter becomes irritating or fearful as the Universe compassionately responds to its desire to become whole.

As the anger, or the fear, within a personality builds, the world in which it lives increasingly reflects the anger, or the fear, that it must heal, so that eventually, ultimately, the personality will see that it is creating its own experiences and perceptions, that its righteous anger or justifiable fear originates within itself, and therefore can be replaced by other perceptions and experiences only through the force of its own being.

Just as the frequency of anger evokes a like frequency in the consciousness of those around an angry personality, the frequency of love awakens also like responses. It is the intention that determines the effect. If what you offer to others is not sensitive, if it does not support and nourish, if it does not empower but disempowers them, it will be met with resistance at some level, and that resistance will be the counterpart of your energy that seeks to disempower, or to control. Separation and distance are always the result of the pursuit of external power.

Within this impersonal framework operate the dynamics of temptation and responsible choice.

The human emotional system can be broken down into roughly two elements: fear and love. Love is of the soul.

Fear is of the personality. The illusion of each personality is generated by and sustained by the emotions that follow fear, such as anger, rage, vengefulness, hatred, jealousy or envy, loneliness, spite, sorrow, despair, grief, regret, greed, lust, arrogance, alienation, self-pity, lethargy, guilt, resentment, and feelings of inferiority and superiority. Emotions such as these lead to corresponding behaviors, such as selfishness—toward people and animals and the Earth and the kingdoms of the Earth—and using others in the many ways that humans use one another—commercially, sexually, emotionally—and lying, manipulation, violence, brutality, impatience, ridicule, and judgment.

When the personality is unconscious, every emotion of fear, or that follows fear, produces a negative behavior, a behavior that creates negative karma for its soul. Each of the emotions that follows fear can cause any of the behaviors that are based upon fear. Jealousy, for example, can result in lying, or in ridicule, which are forms of manipulation, or in violence. Greed can result in impatience, which is a form of selfishness, or judging or using others.

If you are unconscious of the part of yourself that is angry, for example, if you are unaware of yourself as a splintered personality, you will enact the anger of that part of yourself without thinking. You will strike out, or withdraw, or ridicule, or in some way express your anger. Your anger will spill out of your private energy sphere and into the collective energy of those around you, creating negative karma. As you encounter the results of your own anger, as they come back to you through the laws of karma and attraction, you, or another of your soul's personalities, eventually will learn to create differently, and so on for each of the negative emotions that follows fear.

Behind fear is powerlessness. As you reach outward to fill the places within you that are empty of power, you learn, one by one, that those places cannot be filled in that way. Eventually, whether in this lifetime, or after a thousand lifetimes, you will turn toward authentic power. This is the unconscious way of learning. It is learning through the experiences that are created by the unconscious parts of the personality, and through the experiences that are created by unconscious reactions to those experiences.

If a personality is aware of its splintered state, if it is aware not only of the aspect of itself that is angry and demands vengeance, for example, but also of the aspect of itself that is compassionate and understanding, it benefits from the dynamic of temptation. It is able to preview the consequences of identifying with the frequency of energy that is anger that is running through its system, to look them over in advance of living them, and to decide whether they are worth expressing the anger that it feels. It is able to foresee, through its decision to foresee, how expressing the current of anger in that moment will affect itself and the people around it, and also the effects of expressing understanding and compassion.

The unconscious personality is not aware in the moment of its anger or its rage that there are aspects of itself that would prefer to respond with compassion and understanding, but it would recognize them if it could see clearly in that moment. What of the parts of itself that suffer the loneliness and alienation that result from expressing anger, the parts that long for warmth and companionship, for relationships of a depth and quality that are not possible to those who live in anger or fear or jealousy?

If the personality that is tempted decides to align itself with love, with clarity, understanding, and compassion, it gains power. The impulse toward anger, or resentment, or vengeance loses power over it, and in this way, step by step, conscious decision by conscious decision, it becomes truly powerful. If it decides to remain unconscious, to avoid responsibility for its actions, it allows negative currents of energy to form its words and shape its actions. This results in negative behavior, and this results in negative karma.

What does this mean in terms of the illusion?

Negative behavior produces within others and within oneself negative emotions and, therefore, more opportunities to gain power through responsible choice or to create negative karma. Negative karma means that the personality that chooses negative behavior, or another of its soul's personalities, will experience that same negative behavior from another personality, and, again, be given the opportunity to decide to release or continue that mode of learning.

This is the illusion. It is an illusion because you and the other souls that are involved have agreed, in compassion and wisdom, to participate in the learning dynamics of the Earth school in order to heal. It is illusion because within nonphysical reality neither space nor time nor anger nor jealousy nor fear exists. It is an illusion because when you return home it will cease to be.

Therefore, how are you to judge a soul that is involved in this learning process? What step, or steps, do you abstract and say, "This is wrong," "That is worthy," "Here she has succeeded" and "Here he has not"? You cannot judge the learnings of a soul on the basis of how that learning takes place without creating negative karma. In other words, a soul is capable of being examined in process. Just as you can ask yourself, "Where does my anger come from?" and realize that it springs from a multitude of dynamics, some of which were set into motion centuries ago, or longer, and that are only now coming to completion, that it is a current of energy within you that you are seeking to release in order to heal your soul and balance its karmic energy, you cannot try another as if you were a judge in a court for a single angry experience. Rather you would have to see clearly that there is a process unfolding and add to that the factor of karma.

You can only judge that the soul is involved by its own will in a process of healing, and that it is evolving, as are you, and as is the rest of the Universe. This is non-judgmental justice. It is justice that does not judge the process of the soul's evolution except that it recognize with love that the soul is reaching for love.

It is not the way of the Universe to look through the eyes of right and wrong and failure or success. How do you know what "success" is? Can you see in fullness the causes and effects of your being and of your acts and of your words? Therefore, how do you know what success is, and how can you possibly imagine what failure is? What is "failure" but a cause and effect? What we call failure is simply a cause and its effect, simply the process of cause and effect in action. It is wise to imagine the dynamics that we think of as "failure" and "success" as not truly existing, because they do not, not from the position of truth, only from the position of judgment.

How can you say what within the illusion is worthy and what is not? "Unworthiness" is the judgment of not being perfected, but look around you. Do you see perfection completed by each human being, except that they are, in their own process, perfect and worthy? It is the process that is worthy and perfect at all times, and in that you complete the task fully.

How is it possible to know what to pursue within the illusion and what not to pursue?

Ask yourself what is the difference between your essential needs and your adopted needs, or perhaps another term might be artificial needs. What are your genuine needs, and what are the needs that you have created for other reasons, to control, or to maneuver others, or to gain attention? Distinguish these in your mind. Know yourself deeply and clearly enough to recognize what is a legitimate need of you as a human being and of you as that part of yourself that has created needs for certain other reasons—such as to gain external notice, or prestige, or to become a distinguishable individual. Learn to identify these and then choose which you wish to live with.

For example, is your irritation at the neighbor's noise a

result of a genuine need that is going unmet, or a created need? Does your annoyance with the sounds that the garbage truck makes, or your desire to have the clerk at the grocery store treat you politely, reflect an essential need or an artificial one? Learn to distinguish your real needs, what you truly need as a human being and a soul, from the needs that you have adopted for reasons that are based on external power and do not emerge from the needs of your soul. Once you get a clear sense of that you can begin to separate yourself from your artificial self, and then you are in a position to choose clearly how you wish to respond, and to hold yourself accountable when you allow your artificial needs to take over.

Authentic needs belong to the soul. You need, for example, to love and to be loved. You need to express your creativity, whether that is in raising a family or leading a country. You need to cultivate your spirit, to work consciously at aligning your personality with your soul. You need to be counseled with the impersonal wisdom of your nonphysical Teachers, and the guidance of your nonphysical guides. These are some of your authentic needs.

Nonauthentic needs belong to the personality. They are what you adopt in your physical life in order to maneuver the space you claim and walk in upon the Earth. Artificial needs are the needs from which negative karma is incurred. As you reach to fulfill these needs without letting them go and bending and flowing, as you determine to have them satisfied or to use them, you can gain great negative karma.

A nonauthentic need is a barrier. Neither nations nor

individuals need as much as they have. They are artificial barriers, and the purpose behind their formation is the accumulation of external power. The secondary gain, so to speak, behind the creation of artificial needs is artificial power. Look clearly and you will see it everywhere—in marriages, in international relations, in every conflict.

It is not possible for you to experience the complete emergence of your soul when you are clouded over by artificial needs. When that happens all you can see are artificial needs, and you see them as being ever so important, ever so significant, but are they really? As you look at your not-as-authentic needs, can you see how they drain energy from you? So long as your priorities come from your lesser self, you cannot touch your higher self in a direct way.

Authentic needs are the needs that are always met by the Universe. The Universe is that which supplies you with your authentic needs. You are always being given opportunities to love and be loved, for example, yet ask yourself how many times in your life you have squandered these opportunities.

By learning to respond to your authentic needs and by allowing your artificial ones to drop aside as unnecessary defense mechanisms, you become more open and understanding and compassionate with others. There is a natural give and take in the course of every human life. Each human being has authentic and nonauthentic needs, and that is where the natural grit for the flow between us comes from in the living environment. You begin to learn to give and take as you begin to work through an understanding of what your real needs are, and learn to compromise and give and transcend when it comes to the needs of those parts of yourself that are not genuine or do not enhance your development.

If you see clearly through your own authentic needs, you will see that what you are really feeling threatened by when you experience an artificial need is the loss of your power, and, therefore, rather than being able to address it directly, you create an artificial need that does the speaking for you. Learn to address the real need so that you do not have to burden yourself with behavioral patterns that are not true to your own nature, that cloud you, that give you some artificial persona that you have to live up to.

Begin by truly watching your own needs in action—where they are real and where they are not, and where they are not, expect to experience a negative emotion. Work on becoming one step detached from that feeling so that you are no longer blinded by it or unaware that you are feeling it. Become a step away so that you can let it begin to work its way through you without penetrating as deeply as it does in terms of creating action and negative thoughts and emotional withdrawals and all the other reactions it creates within you. Become one step detached from it, and every time that you are able to see it you will become more and more and more detached.

You will begin to be able to see the illusion in motion, and that is a part of authentic power.*

---

* To learn how to apply what you have learned in this chapter and deepen your experiences, see the Chapter 14 Study Guide on page 317.

— 15 —

Power

What is the nature of power? What does it mean to be a truly powerful human being?

Power is not the ability to exert your will upon another person. There is no inner security in that kind of power. That is an attribute of time, and as time changes, that changes, too. Do you have a strong body that others cannot challenge? That will change. What will you do then? Do you have a physical beauty that can be used to influence others? That will change. What will you do then? Do you have a cleverness that maneuvers others? What happens when you are too tired to use it, or you miss the opportunity?

If you are not at home in the world, you live in the fear of one who can never truly relax and enjoy Life. Is this power?

There is no power in fear, or in any of the activities that are generated by fear. There is no power in a thought form of fear, even if it is supported by armies. The armies of Rome disappeared more than a millennium ago, but the force of the life of a single human that Roman soldiers put to death continues to shape the development of our species. Who had the power?

You are only as powerful as that for which you stand. Do you stand for more money in the bank and a bigger house? Do you stand for an attractive mate? Do you stand for imposing your way of thinking upon others? These are the stands of the personality seeking to satisfy its wants. Do you stand for perfection, for the beauty and compassion of each soul? Do you stand for the power of love and the clarity of wisdom? Do you stand for forgiveness and humbleness? These are the stands of the personality that has aligned itself with its soul. This is the position of a truly powerful personality.

Power is energy that is formed by the intentions of the soul. It is Light shaped by the intentions of love and compassion guided by wisdom. It is energy that is focused and directed toward the fulfillment of the tasks of the soul upon the Earth, and the development of the personality as a physical instrument of the soul that is appropriate to those tasks. It is the force that shapes the illusion into the images of the souls that are creating it, and not those of their personalities.

What does this mean?

There is a continual energy exchange between souls. This exchange is splintered when the personality is splintered.

Energy, power, leaves a splintered personality through each of its different parts. If one part of you fears the loss of your job, and another fears the loss of a relationship, and another dreads confrontation with an unpleasant co-worker, power flows from you without your conscious control. This is how the energy dynamics of an unempowered personality work.

When energy leaves you in fear or distrust, it cannot bring you anything but discomfort or pain. When energy flows from your system in fear or distrust, you experience a physical feeling of pain or discomfort in the part of your body that is associated with the particular energy center that is losing power. When you fear for your ability to protect and care for yourself in the world, to pay your rent, for example, or to keep yourself safe from physical or emotional harm—when you see power as external and you feel that you do not have enough of it to insure your well-being or your safety—you experience discomfort or pain in the area of your stomach, in the area of your solar plexus. What we call anxiety is the experience of power leaving through the energy center that is located in this area of the body. An anxiety attack is a massive loss of power from your system through that energy center. Power losses affect the surrounding parts of the body. Power loss through this center, for example, can cause indigestion. If it is chronic or acute, it can ulcerate the stomach.

When you fear that your ability to love or to be loved is threatened, when you fear, for example, expressing your own love or receiving love from another, you experience physical discomfort or pain in the region of your chest, near your heart. What we experience, literally, as heartache is the experience of power leaving in fear or distrust through this energy center. Have you lost a mate, or a child, or someone very dear to you? Sort through your experience. Determine what it is that you felt. You will discover that your body hurt, that you were in pain in the vicinity of your chest. That is the experience of power leaving through that energy center. That is what a heartache is, the loss of power through your heart center. Chronic or acute loss of power through the heart center results, literally, in an attack of the heart. There is more to myocardial infarction, to heart attack, than cholesterol in the blood and other conditions of the physical system.

Every distress and every dysfunction of the physical body, every illness, can be understood in terms of power loss to an external circumstance or object through one of several energy centers within the body. You lose power when you rage against an injustice. You lose power when you are threatened by another person, or other people. You lose power when you distance yourself from your fellow humans out of resentment or bitterness, or a sense of disappointment or unworthiness or superiority. You lose power when you long for something or someone, when you grieve, and when you envy another. Beneath all of these is fear, fear that you are vulnerable, that you are not able to cope without the person or the situation that you miss, that you are at a disadvantage without that which you envy. You lose power whenever you fear. That is what a loss of power is.

You do not stop losing power by refusing to recognize your fear, by anesthetizing yourself to what you feel. The road to authentic power is always through what you feel, through your heart. The way of the heart is one of compassion and emotional perception. Therefore, it is never appropriate to suppress an emotion, or to disregard what you feel. If you do not know what you feel, you cannot come to know the splintered nature of your personality, and to challenge those aspects and those energies that do not serve your development.

By remaining in your power you do not become a static energy system, one that hoards energy to itself. You become a stable energy system, capable of conscious acts of focus and intention. You become a magnet for those who are illumined and those who want to be. At issue is the manner in which energy flows from you. When energy leaves you in any way except in strength and trust, it cannot bring back to you anything but pain and discomfort. An authentically empowered human being, therefore, is a human being that does not release its energy except in love and trust.

What are the characteristics of an authentically empowered human being?

An authentically empowered person is humble. This does not mean the false humility of one who stoops to be with those who are below him or her. It is the inclusiveness of one who responds to the beauty of each soul, who sees in each personality and in the actions of each personality the soul incarnate upon the Earth. It is the harmlessness of one who treasures and honors and reveres Life in all its forms. Are you concerned for the Earth? It is the humble who have never harmed the Earth.

What does it mean to be harmless?

It means being so strong that you need not harm a creature. That is what it means: you are so able and empowered that the idea of showing power through harm is not even a part of your consciousness. Without genuine humility, you cannot have this kind of power because power leaves you when you feel that the situation that you are in, or the people that you are with, do not command your respect.

A humble spirit walks a familiar world. People are not strangers to it; they are its companions upon the Earth. A humble spirit does not ask for more than it needs, and what it needs, the Universe provides. A humble spirit is content with the fulfillment of its authentic needs, and is not burdened with artificial needs.

Humble spirits are free to love and to be who they are. They have no artificial standards to live up to. They are not drawn to the symbols of external power. They do not compete for external power. This does not mean that they do not take pride in what they can do well, or that they do not focus their efforts to produce the best that they can, or are not spurred onward by their fellow humans when that is appropriate to the situation.

To compete means to strive for something in company or together, to aim at something, to try to reach something, to seek after something with others. If the something that you aim for is prestige or notice or a gold medal instead of a tin medal, it is your personality that is motivating the competition. You are striving to empower yourself at the expense of others, to assert your superiority over another, or over other human beings. You are striving for external power. By striving for this reward and that reward, you ask the world to assess and acknowledge your value before you can value yourself. You place your sense of self-worth in the hands of others. You have no power even if you win every gold medal that the world can produce.

If what you seek is the joy of giving without reservation, of giving with purpose and joy and consciousness all that you have to the effort that you and other souls are creating jointly, your competition is the expression of your soul. When the effort that finishes last in time has the same value as the effort that finishes first, when the quality of the immortal, timeless soul is honored instead of the time-bound personality and body, when your giving is not impeded by fear of vulnerability, when the size or color or shape of what you receive or do not receive does not matter, you will know the power of a humble spirit.

An authentically empowered person is one who forgives. Forgiveness is not a moral issue. It is an energy dynamic. When most people forgive they do not want those that they forgave to forget that they forgave and forgot. This kind of forgiveness manipulates the person who is forgiven. It is not forgiveness. It is a means of acquiring external power over another.

Forgiveness means that you do not carry the baggage of an experience. When you choose not to forgive, the experience that you do not forgive sticks with you. When you choose not to forgive, it is like agreeing to wear dark, gruesome sunglasses that distort everything, and it is you who are forced every day to look at Life through those contaminated lenses because you have chosen to keep them. You wish everyone else to see the world that way because you wish to see the world that way, and it is indeed the world that you are looking at, but it is only you who sees it. You are looking through the lenses of your own contaminated love.

Forgiveness means that you do not hold others responsible for your experiences. If you do not hold yourself accountable for what you experience, you will hold someone else accountable, and if you are not satisfied with what you experience, you will seek to change it by manipulating that person. Complaining, for example, is exactly that dynamic of wanting someone to be responsible for what you experience, and to fix things for you.

Complaining is a form of manipulation, but you are free to move beyond that into the next step, which is perception and sharing without manipulation. What is at stake is not your sharing, but the intention behind it. When complaining is used instead of sharing, that is what becomes negative, but not the sharing. It is how you cast the sharing, or shape it, before—the intention with which you share. Before you share, ask yourself, "What is my intention in sharing this?

Am I looking for a particular response?" Use this as a way of centering your attitude before committing energy to words. When you assume responsibility for what you experience and share what you experience in a spirit of companionship, that is the same as forgiveness.

When you hold someone responsible for what you experience, you lose power. You cannot know what another person will do. Therefore, when you depend upon another person for the experiences that you think are necessary to your well-being, you live continually in the fear that they will not deliver. The perception that someone else is responsible for what you experience underlies the idea that forgiveness is something that one person does for another. How can you forgive another person for the fact that you have chosen to step out of your power?

When you forgive you release critical judgment of yourself as well as of others. You lighten up. You do not cling to negative experiences that resulted from decisions that you made while you were learning. That is regret. Regret is the double negativity of clinging to negativity. You lose power when you regret. If one person grieves at his or her experiences while another is able to laugh, who is the lighter? Which is harmless? The heart that dances is the innocent heart. The one that cannot laugh is burdened. It is the dancing heart that is harmless.

This does not mean that you do not learn from what you have experienced, and apply that in each moment as you make your decisions. That is responsible choice. If you are doing all that you can to the fullest of your ability as well as you can, there is nothing else that is asked of a soul.

An authentically empowered human being is clear in his or her perceptions and thinking. Clarity is the perception of wisdom. It is seeing with wisdom. It is being able to perceive and understand the illusion, and to let it play. It is being able to see beyond the activities of the personality to the force of the immortal soul. It is being able to understand what it is that is striving to come into being—the health and integration of the personality and the evolution of the soul. It is the ability to recognize nonphysical dynamics as they appear within the world of time and matter. It is understanding the laws of karma and attraction and their relationship to what you experience. It is being able to see the role of responsible choice and choosing accordingly in each moment.

Clarity is the ability to see the soul in action in the physical world. It results from choosing to learn through wisdom instead of through fear and doubt. Clarity allows you to experience your fellow humans with compassion instead of with judgment. Can you not see the karma that another is creating for himself or herself by choosing the currents of anger or greed? Have you not made the same choices yourself? Have you not felt vulnerable? Have you not struck out at others? Clarity brings forth true compassion, the sharing of passion with others. It allows the energy of the heart to flow.

Clarity turns pain into suffering. It sees the dynamic of the personality that is the cause of the pain, and the relationship of that dynamic and that experience to the evolution of the soul. It is the perception in each moment that everything is designed for wholeness and perfection, and every aspect serves ultimately a beautiful learning. An authentically empowered personality sees the perfection of each situation and each experience for the evolution of each soul and the maturation of each personality involved. It sees perfection in the smallest details everywhere. Wherever it looks, it sees the hand of God.

Clarity evaporates fear. It allows you to choose the vertical path and to stay on it. It allows you to understand the dynamics beneath your addictions—what your addictions serve and how they operate—and to make the choices that will disempower them and empower you. It allows you to challenge not merely a force that you do not understand, such as attraction to alcohol, or a drug, or indiscriminate sex, but a dynamic that you understand in terms of its causes and its effects. It allows you to choose consciously, and to know why you are choosing as you do.

Clarity allows you to see the world of physical matter for what it is, a learning environment that is created jointly by the intentions of the souls that share it. Therefore, it allows you to recognize the effects of the intentions that shape the personal reality of each human at work at levels of reality that are created jointly. It allows you to see, for example, the extent to which relationships between nations have been shaped by the energy of the personality and the extent to which they have been shaped by the energy of the soul, and to recognize that the energy of the soul is entirely lacking at this level, and at most others.

Clarity allows you to see that the decision-making process within the human condition is linked to the evolution of others, and in what way. It allows you to see that you participate in the evolution of joint energy dynamics, such as the archetypes—the collective human ideas—of sacred partnership, male, female, wife, and priest through the decisions that you make. It allows you to see that your contribution to the evolution of your soul is precisely the decisions that you make at each moment, and that those decisions are embodied in the physical reality that you share with your fellow humans.

An authentically empowered person lives in love. Love is the energy of the soul. Love is what heals the personality. There is nothing that cannot be healed by love. There is nothing but love.

Love is not a passive state. It is an active force. It is the force of the soul. Love does more than bring peace where there is conflict. It brings a different way of being in the world. It brings harmony and an active interest in the wellbeing of others. It brings concern and care. It brings Light. It washes away the concerns of the personality. In the Light of love there is only love.

There is a relationship between love and power and the transformation of the quality of experiences that occur within the Earth school as a whole. The type of power that you are trying to transform in yourself is the type of power that needs to be transformed in general upon the Earth. There are numerous, numerous, numerous human beings who are drawn to violence—violent fantasies and violent acts. Most of them essentially center in the fact that the individual himself or herself feels powerless and victimized and, therefore, wants to live, for a brief period of time with one other human being, a sense of being empowered, but there is no genuine power to be found in that area.

It is through the evolution of your own consciousness, through focusing on more and more empowered choices, that you create the distance that is necessary between you and your negative emotions, and heal yourself in such a way that violence no longer asserts itself. To heal violence there must be love.

Love is the energy of the soul, and, therefore, the experience of giving and receiving love, of living a life of love, fulfills the personality. It is something that the personality continually reaches for. Reaching for love unconsciously can produce anger and fear. This happens when the personality does not see clearly what it is reaching for, which is the case with addiction.

If you reach for an addictive sexual relationship, for example, you are reaching for love. It is the illusion that you think that you are reaching for something so manly or womanly. You are reaching for love, but you will not admit it and will not deal with it, so there is anger within you because there is a level of energy and emotion that longs to be born but is never given an outlet.

It is emotionally, spiritually impossible to have a sexual connection with a human being and not ignite certain emotional patterns, but they are a continual dead-end street when there is no relationship or true emotional feelings to go with the act. Therefore, there is a level of brutality, frustration, and eventually emotional disease which results in physical illness and breakdown because a significant pattern is being tremendously abused. Remember, you do get what you ask for.

Asking for love is asking for the energy of the soul. It brings with it a genuine concern for the other. You cannot prey upon someone whose well-being is in your heart.

When you seek to impose your intelligence or your way of seeing upon another, you are reaching for love, but you are routing your reach, so to speak, through the wants of your personality. You are seeking external power. There is only emptiness there. When you seek to dominate another you dominate no one but disempower yourself. The less empowered you feel, the more you feel a need to control that which is external. The loving personality seeks not to control, but to nurture, not to dominate, but to empower. Love is the richness and fullness of your soul flowing through you.

Humbleness, forgiveness, clarity, and love are the dynamics of freedom. They are the foundations of authentic power.*

---

* To learn how to apply what you have learned in this chapter and deepen your experiences, see the Chapter 15 Study Guide on page 322.

— 16 —

Trust

Each soul comes to the Earth with gifts. A soul does not incarnate only to heal and to balance its energy, to pay its karmic debts, but also to contribute its specialness in specific ways. Each soul brings the particular configuration of the Life force that it is to the needs of the Earth school. It does this with purpose and intention.

Before it incarnates, each soul agrees to perform certain tasks upon the Earth. It enters into a sacred agreement with the Universe to accomplish specific goals. It enters into this commitment in the fullness of its being. That is why when a soul succeeds in accomplishing its goal, in fulfilling what it has agreed to do, there is a richness and a specialness to the lifetime of that personality that is recognized and honored by its fellow souls, both physical and nonphysical.

Each soul takes upon itself a particular task. It may be the task of raising a family, or communicating ideas through writing, or transforming the consciousness of a community, such as the business community. It may be the task of awakening the awareness of the power of love at the level of nations, or even contributing directly to the evolution of consciousness on a global level. Whatever the task that your soul has agreed to, whatever its contract with the Universe, all of the experiences of your life serve to awaken within you the memory of that contract, and to prepare you to fulfill it.

An unempowered personality cannot complete the task of its soul. It languishes in an inner sense of emptiness. It seeks to fill itself with external power, but that will not satisfy it. This sense of emptiness, or something missing, or of something wrong, cannot be healed by satisfying the wants of the personality. Gratifying needs that are based upon fear will not bring you to the touchstone of purpose. No matter how successful the personality becomes in accomplishing its goals, those goals will not be enough. Eventually it will hunger for the energy of its soul. Only when the personality begins to walk the path that its soul has chosen will it satisfy its hunger.

Authentic empowerment and the fulfillment of the soul's task upon the Earth, therefore, are not separate dynamics. Authentic empowerment is necessary to accomplish fully the mission of the soul, yet as you move into authentic empowerment, you move toward the fulfillment of your soul's agreement with the Universe, and as you move toward that fulfillment—as you move consciously toward the energy of your soul—you empower yourself. You and the work of your soul upon the Earth expand together. As one grows and develops, so does the other.

When a soul incarnates, its memory of the agreement that it has made with the Universe becomes soft. It becomes dormant, awaiting the experiences that will activate it. These experiences are not necessarily experiences that the personality would choose. They are nonetheless necessary to the activation of the awareness of the power and the mission of the soul within the consciousness of the personality, and to its preparation for that task.

What does it feel like to remember your soul's task?

When the deepest part of you becomes engaged in what you are doing, when your activities and actions become gratifying and purposeful, when what you do serves both yourself and others, when you do not tire within but seek the sweet satisfaction of your life and your work, you are doing what you were meant to be doing. The personality that is engaged in the work of its soul is buoyant. It is not burdened with negativity. It does not fear. It experiences purposefulness and meaning. It delights in its work and in others. It is fulfilled and fulfilling.

Interactions with your parents, and with those whom you have chosen to share your intimacy, and with those with whom—out of the billions of souls upon our planet—you share parts of your life, serve to activate within you an awareness of who you are and what you are here to do. The pains that you suffer, the lonelinesses that you encounter, the experiences that are disappointing or distressing, the addictions and seeming pitfalls of your life are each doorways to awareness. Each offers you an opportunity to see beyond the illusion that serves the balancing and growth of your soul.

Within each experience of pain or negativity is the opportunity to challenge the perception that lies behind it, the fear that lies behind it, and to choose to learn with wisdom. The fear will not vanish immediately, but it will disintegrate as you work with courage. When fear ceases to scare you, it cannot stay. When you choose to learn through wisdom, to evolve consciously, your fears surface one at a time in order for you to exorcise them with inner faith. That is how it happens. You exorcise your own demons.

Your guides and Teachers continually offer you Light. They encourage you in each moment to your fullest growth and development, yet they cannot prevent you from your learning or your growing or your moving through your experiences and letting your experiences influence you. This is so even if you are able to communicate with them consciously and directly. Your experiences will move you right or left, and you will ask your Teacher this question or that. If you move left, your question will be entirely different than if you had moved right, and the reality that you open by that question will be entirely different.

There is no single optimal path for the soul. There are many optimal paths. With each choice you immediately create numerous paths within a choice, one of which is then optimal. In other words, the optimal path of your soul is the choice of awareness, the vertical path. Once you have made that choice, then come the various forms of enactment.

In what way, therefore, does nonphysical guidance serve you?

It is a partnership of challenging you to come to terms with the full width and breadth and depth of authentic power and responsible choice. It is not that you give permission to be mindlessly manipulated. It is that you give permission to be shown the fullest of your power and guided to its use.

When you depend entirely upon the ability of your personality to determine what is best for you, you may stand in the way of a richness that is waiting for you. How do you know what the Universe has waiting for you if you take off your restrictions? If you are determined to have your life unfold in a particular way, and none other—if you have your heart set on using your creativity only to accumulate money, for example—consider that you build your entire reality around that. The Universe cannot help you in the same way that it can if you are trusting of it, because it cannot overshadow nor penetrate your choice. Yet what if what you are doing is more appropriately regarded in a social sphere rather than an economic one? In other words, what if the enterprise that you seek to develop is more appropriately a way to an avenue that you have not yet recognized? It is now deadlocked because it cannot go down its appropriate path, for you have your hand on a door that you insist upon opening that will go nowhere.

Can you see?

Let go of what you think is just reward. Let go. Trust. Create. Be who you are. The rest is up to your nonphysical Teachers and the Universe.

Take your hands off the steering wheel. Be able to say to the Universe, "Thy will be done," and to know it within your intentions. Spend time in this thought. Consider what it means to say, "Thy will be done," and allow your life to go into the hands of the Universe completely. The final piece of reaching for authentic power is releasing your own to a higher form of wisdom.

Long before we, as a species, became aware that there is such a dimension as the realm of nonphysical guidance and Teachers, each human being was guided, and beautifully, by many nonphysical Teachers. Even though unseen by us, this guidance happened nonetheless in its perfection and in its balance. That is what is happening now. It is just that for the first time, as we become multisensory, we are aware of it, and can put names with nonphysical Teachers and have a sense of personal relationship with them, yet still it is that what you experience is always appropriate and will always move toward the greatest wisdom of your development and guidance.

Remind yourself that you are supported, that you are not going it alone upon this Earth. Dwell in the company of your nonphysical Teachers and guides. Do not discriminate in terms of what you can and should ask and speak about.

Just assume and live in the beauty of the bond. Do not fear dependency. What is wrong with being dependent upon the Universe, whether that is your Teachers or Divine Intelligence? You do what you do for yourself and the Universe and your nonphysical Teachers and guides are there in assistance. They will never do it for you. It is not possible for them to do it for you. Delight in the dependency. Give your guides and Teachers permission to come closer.

When you ask for guidance and assistance, simply assume that it immediately is pouring forward. You may need to work awhile to relax your mind into receptivity, or you may need to have lunch, or drive into town or do whatever it is that you need to do in order to relax your mind to hear or to feel, but live in the total assumption that the moment that you ask for guidance it is pouring in.

Try looking at life as a beautifully well-organized dynamic. Trust the Universe. Trusting means that the circumstance that you are in is working toward your best and most appropriate end. There is no when to that. There is no if to that. It is. Release your specifications and say to the Universe: "Find me where you know I need to be." Let them go and trust that the Universe will provide, and so it shall. Let go of all. Let your higher self complete its task.

Allow yourself to pray. Just as the many times human beings find themselves in circumstances where the hurt or the pain is so great that on their own power they cannot forgive, it is enough that they pray to be given the grace, the perception, the elevated Light that will allow them to forgive.

It is impossible for you to come full circle in this way of

empowerment without prayer. It is not enough to want or to intend or to meditate. You must pray. You must talk. You must ask. You must believe. That is partnership.

Think of what you are doing as entering into partnership with Divine Intelligence, a partnership in which you begin to share your concerns with the understanding that there is an Intelligence receptive to what you are saying that helps you create within your own environment of matter and energy the most effective dynamics to bring you into wholeness. You do not need to think that you create alone, but rather that you are guided strongly in ways to help cocreate in the most effective way for your healing and for the fulfillment of your contract.

Consider your intentions and your meditations as part of what is done within the context of prayer. Be able to say within your intentions and your meditations, "And I ask for guidance or help," and expect to get it. Expect to get it. Aside from your level of the responsible choice of energy and how you form that into matter, the dependency on prayer assists you in pulling to yourself and invoking grace. Prayer is moving into a personal relationship with Divine Intelligence.

It is impossible to have a prayer without power. It is impossible to have a thought that is a secret, for all energy is heard. When you pray, you draw to you and invoke grace. Grace is uncontaminated conscious Light. It is Divinity. Prayer brings grace and grace calms you. That is the cycle. Grace is the tranquilizer of the soul. With grace comes a knowing that what you are experiencing is necessary. It calms you with a sense of knowing.

Relax into the present moment. Do what you need to do in the present moment. Yours is not to worry about that which we call the future. That does not mean that you do not consider the consequences of each of your choices. Taking into account the consequences of your decisions is responsible choice. It means to create strongly in the present moment. Do not lose power over the what-ifs of your life. These are unlimited and endless. Keep your power in the now, in present time. Keep your power just in the day that you are living on the Earth, and not on how to maneuver tomorrow.

Use all of your worldly connections, but not out of panic and not out of fear. Do what you need to do on your end. Your choice comes in knowing appropriate timing, clear motivation, and trust. Allow your intuition to guide your timing. Take it inside, ask how you feel, and then move forward. Allow yourself to experience what it is to learn step by step the freedom that comes from being unattached to the outcome, but operating from an empowered heart.

Do not assume that the Universe operates like humankind, because it does not. Do not insist that the Universe comply with your understanding of it. Rather hold on to the thought that there is nothing without value that exists upon the Earth, that it is impossible to create any form of Life that does not have value. Therefore, it is impossible to create any action that does not have value. You may not see it, but that is irrelevant. Live in the trust that when it is appropriate, pieces will fall into place and you will see clearly.

Trust allows you to call forth your negativities in order to heal them. It allows you to follow your feelings through your defenses to their sources, and to bring to the Light of consciousness those aspects of yourself that resist wholeness, that live in fear. The journey to authentic power requires that you become conscious of all that you feel. The unearthing and healing of your negativities may appear to be an endless process, but it is not. Your vulnerabilities and weaknesses and fears are not different from those of your fellow humans. Do not despair because your humanness awakens.

Feel your intentions in your heart. Feel not what your mind tells you, but what your heart tells you. Rather than serve the fake gods of your mind, serve your heart, the real God. You will not find God in your intellect. Divine Intelligence is in the heart.

Open yourself to your fellow humans. Allow yourself to experience what you feel toward them, and to hear what they feel. Your interactions with them form the basis of your growth. When you fear what you will find in yourself, or what you will find in others, if you allow yourself to hear what others have to say, you turn your back on the opportunities that the Universe is giving you to find the power of your heart, the power of compassion. It is not until you have the courage to engage in human relationships that you grow.

Compassion is mutual compassion. The physical body is soothed and invigorated by the energy of the heart, and torn by lower-frequency currents of anger, rage, fear, and violence. When you treat another harshly and distance yourself from your heart, it is you that suffers as well as the other, and when you treat another with compassion, you treat yourself kindly at the same time. As your consciousness expands, and as you become aware of what you feel, you become aware of the dual effects of compassion and the lack of it. You become aware of the damage that you do to your own body when you feel and act without compassion.

Challenge your fears. Fear of growing and of transformation of self is what causes you to want to disengage from the present situation and reach for another. When you feel that you are in a pattern of wanting what you do not have instead of what you do have, of seeing the grass in the other pasture as greener because it is in the other pasture, confront it. Challenge it each time that it comes up by literally realizing that when it comes up you are not in the present moment, you are not engaged in your present energy dynamic but, rather, you are letting energy leak to a future that does not exist.

Each time you feel negative, stop, acknowledge that you are, and discharge it consciously. Ask what you are feeling and what is at the root of it. Go for the root of it in that instant and, as you work to pull the root, simultaneously look at the positive side and remind yourself of the greater truth that there is something spiritually profound at work, that your life is no accident, that you are under contract.

Be mindful of the words that you use and the actions that

you live and who you are and how it is you use your power. In other words, as you say what you say, as you make commitments, as you form the power of your life, keep clear at all times that you are what you say you are, that you put your force behind what you say, and monitor that accordingly. If you are unaware of your intention, or if you suspect that you are operating from a second agenda, ask yourself, "What is really going on?" Check your motivations. That automatically engages guidance. You will not be alone in your assessment.

Trust allows you to give. Giving is abundant. As you give so it shall be given to you. If you give with judgment, limitation, and stinginess, that is what you will create in your life—judgment, limitation, and stinginess. What you say to others shall be done exactly unto you. That is the law of karma, and how you love and serve others shall be done exactly unto you. If you radiate love and compassion, you do receive it. If you radiate fear and suspicion and a sense of wishing to keep people at arm's length, then negativity comes to you because that is what you are asking for.

Trust allows the experience of bliss. When you trust that the Universe in each moment is providing for the needs of your soul, and that the guidance and assistance of your non-physical guides and Teachers are always available to you, you are free to enjoy your interactions with others and to leave aside the heavier frequencies of manipulation and protectiveness. Awakeness is a blissful state, not a painful one. It is blissful. It is fully balanced and lovingly harmonious. It is all of these things and more. The vertical path means clarity, not pain.

Trust allows you to laugh. You can just as easily laugh and play while you grow as become serious and overwhelmed. Spiritual partners see from the perspective of the impersonal, and they help each other see from that perspective the meaning of their experiences. They can laugh at the richness and the beauty and the playfulness of the Universe. They enjoy each other. They see the frustrations of the wants of the personality for what they are, learnings, sometimes great learnings, for the soul.

All of what you are doing in each day is creating what is appropriate and perfect. Apply consciousness to this process. That is trust. Although what you encounter and what you do in each moment is appropriate and perfect to the evolution of your soul, the shape of the experiences of your life is determined nonetheless by the choices that you make. It is you that chooses to linger in resentment, or to be consumed by anger, or enveloped in grief, or to release these lower-frequency currents of energy. Each choice that you make, to dwell in negativity or to take up residence in your heart, serves perfectly the evolution of your soul. All roads lead to home.

If you choose anger, or grief, or resentment, or jealousy you will learn the lesson of love, but you will learn it through pain and trauma and a sense of loss. You will not not evolve. This is not possible. You are on a quest for authentic power. You cannot give up this quest. Your only choice is whether you wish to have the quest consciously or unconsciously. You can choose through your responses to life's difficulties to engage the full power of your soul. This is the conscious path to authentic empowerment.

If you will eventually evolve beyond the Earth school, beyond the need for a personality and a body and the illusion in which fear and anger and insecurity appear to exist, why should you choose the vertical path?

This is for you to decide. The path that you now walk is not unknown to the Universe. The pains and distresses and violences that you experience can be considered as signposts along the path that you have chosen. If you have chosen the path of learning through jealousy, for example, you will experience anxiety and fear of loss of what you think you cannot live without because these experiences are part of the path of learning through jealousy. They might be thought of as what that road looks like between mile twenty and mile thirty. If you choose the path of learning through anger, you will experience rejection and violence; if you choose the path of love, you will experience being loved by others, and so on, because the choice of a particular path is also the choice of particular types of experiences. You do not break new ground from the point of view of the Universe.

Whether you continue the quest for external power, which now leads nowhere, or decide to build within yourself authentic power and align yourself with the evolutionary path that our species is now on determines the experiences that you will contribute to the evolution of your soul and to the soul of humankind. You contribute appropriately and perfectly to your evolution and to the evolution of others no matter what you choose. This is true. Yet why choose to learn unconsciously? Have you gained the sense of security and contentment and fulfillment that you seek in this way?

What is it that you wish to contribute and to experience as our species, and as each of us individually, makes the evolutionary transition from the five-sensory perception of the Universe to the multisensory, from evolution through the five-sensory exploration of physical reality to evolution through responsible choice with the guidance and assistance of nonphysical guides and Teachers? Are you comfortable with the thought that the Universe is alien and dead and no more than your five senses can detect? How does your heart respond to the thought that the Universe is alive and compassionate and that with it and with other souls of great power and Light you learn through the process of cocreating the reality that you experience?

Look at the probable futures that are unfolding before our world that is built upon the energy of the personality, and the probable futures that would unfold before a world that is built upon the energy of the soul. Which do you choose?

Allow yourself to become aware of what you feel. Give yourself permission to choose the most positive behavior in each moment. As you discharge negative energy consciously and set your intentions according to what your heart tells you, as you challenge and release your fears and choose to heal, you align your personality with your soul and move toward becoming a being of the Light, fully whole and empowered and inwardly secure. Humbleness, forgiveness, clarity and love, all the gifts of the spirit, take root and bloom, and you draw to yourself the Universe's greatest gift: human beings with open hearts.

Rather than a soul in a body, become a body in a soul. Reach for your soul. Reach even farther. The impulse of creation and power authentic—the hourglass point between energy and matter: that is the seat of the soul. What does it mean to touch that place?

It is exciting to come of age spiritually.*

---

* To learn how to apply what you have learned in this chapter and deepen your experiences, see the Chapter 16 Study Guide on page 327.

An Invitation

Dear Friend,

If you are interested in creating authentic power and spiritual partnerships in your life, I invite you to join me at Seatofthe Soul.com. It contains a wealth of information, resources, tips, and practical exercises to support you in creating a life filled with joy, inner peace, and meaningful relationships.

It is the perfect companion to *The Seat of the Soul* and will help you expand into the fullness of your potential and give the gifts you were born to give.

I look forward to seeing you online at SeatoftheSoul.com.

Love,
Gary Zukav

The Seat of the Soul
Study Guide

T*he Seat of the Soul* presents the largest picture possible—
of an entire species transforming from a limited perception
and brutal means of evolution into awareness of itself and
its world as wondrous and spiritual growth as its means of
evolution.

This Study Guide will help you experience this transformation in terms of your own life and everyday experiences.
Its exercises support you in looking at and appreciating
yourself, your experiences, and others in new ways. It suggests experiments to deepen your understanding and ways to
apply it. It encourages you to become the authority in your
life and to see for yourself how to create a life of harmony,
cooperation, sharing, and reverence for Life.

You can explore any question or remain with any exercise
as long as you choose. You can also return to sections to get
deeper insight. I have been exploring my spiritual growth
for about twenty-five years, and I continue to understand

the concepts in *The Seat of the Soul* more deeply each year, sometimes each week. The deeper you allow yourself to go with yourself and others, the more you will accelerate your growth and become a conscious heart-centered contributor to your evolution and the evolution of our species.

Keep a journal while you are studying *The Seat of the Soul*. Each time you read it, you may find deeper meanings and new insights. Write your insights and thoughts in your journal to help you remember them, and also so that you can see over time how they have changed.

You can use this Study Guide alone or with a group. If you study with a group, I suggest you share your answers to the questions and the results of your experiments with your group, if you feel comfortable. The people in your group are your potential spiritual partners. Eventually, new perceptions and values will bring you naturally into constructive cocreation with others. Although no one can do the work of your own evolution for you, the day of the lone wolf, the solitary monk, the hermit seeking enlightenment in isolation is over. Until recently our evolution has unfolded very slowly. Now it is happening at lightning speed. Within a few generations, all humans will experience the expanded perception that is emerging in millions of us. This Study Guide will help you not only to recognize this expanded perception in yourself but also to use it consciously to bring its amazing new potential—authentic power—into your own life.

An expanded version of this Study Guide, including videos and meditations, is available to you online by tapping www.seatofthesoul.com/sg if you are reading an eBook or by typing it into a browser if you are reading a print book. An online support program and community are also available at www.seatofthesoul.com.

I am happy to be a student in the Earth school with you.

Gary Zukav

— Chapter 1 —

The *Seat of the Soul* is about the birth of a new humanity. This birth is part effortless and part challenging. The emergence of multisensory perception—perception beyond what can be seen, heard, tasted, touched, and smelled—is effortless. It is happening whether or not we ask for it. Some people even resist it because they do not want to see what they see. Multisensory perception brings with it a new potential. This is the potential of authentic power. Authentic power is the alignment of the personality with the soul. This new potential does not automatically come into being. Each of us must create it for ourselves. Creating authentic power requires experiencing within us the differences between fear and love and choosing love no matter what is going on inside us—such as anger, jealousy, or resentment—or what is going on outside us—such as another 9/11 attack, an illness, or the death of a child. This is the challenging part. *The Seat of the Soul* shows you what authentic power is, why it is important, and how to create it.

— Evolution —

When the physical environment is seen only from the five-sensory point of view, physical survival appears to be the fundamental criterion of evolution, and the basis of life in the physical arena becomes fear. Power to control the environment and those within it appears to be essential. This produces a type of competition that affects every aspect of our lives. Power over what can be felt, smelled, tasted, heard, or seen is external power. All perceptions of lesser and greater personal value result from the perception of power as external. Competition for external power lies at the heart of all violence. Our deeper understanding leads us to another kind of power that loves Life in every form, does not judge, and perceives meaningfulness and purpose in the smallest details upon the Earth. This is authentic power. Authentic power has its roots in the deepest source of our being. It cannot be bought, inherited, or hoarded. We are evolving from a species that pursues external power into a species that pursues authentic power. No understanding of evolution is adequate that does not have at its core that we are on a journey toward authentic power, and that authentic empowerment is the goal of our evolutionary process and the purpose of our being.

If you are reading an eBook, click the following link to go to an expanded online version of this Chapter Study Guide, including video, meditation, and support for study groups. If you are reading a print copy, type it into your browser: www.seatofthesoul.com/sg1.

Questions

Here are some questions to ask yourself. Open to answers that come to you, and when more thoughts come to you, open yourself to them, also. There are no right or wrong answers. These questions are designed to help you explore yourself and your experiences. Sometimes answers will continue to come to you. Let that happen. If you are in a group, share your answers, and then continue to ask these questions to yourself after you leave the group. Write your answers down so that you will remember them. They will stimulate even more questions and answers in you when you read them in the future.

1. *Do you think that a loving person is more evolved than a mean-spirited person? Why?*
2. *Have you ever had a multisensory experience, or do you think you might have had one?*
3. *Do you ever feel, or suspect, that you have gifts to give, and you want to know what they are?*
4. *What makes a powerful person powerful? Who affects your life most powerfully—people who intimidate you or people who sincerely care for you?*
5. *Write down several examples of external power. Have you had an experience or experiences of authentic power? Write them down.*
6. *Have you ever felt that you are more than you thought you were—for example, more than a mind and a body?*

Exercise

Am I Multisensory?

Make a list of the ways you can identify that you are multisensory. For example:

- *I know inside what decision I need to make.*
- *I have hunches.*
- *I value my insights.*
- *I use my intuition.*
- *Sometimes I know more than I can see.*

(from *The Mind of the Soul* by Gary Zukav and Linda Francis)

Life Lessons

You may be surprised at how much multisensory perception is already a part of your life. The goal is to recognize it, honor it, and experiment with it. Experiences of multisensory perception may be more natural to you than you expect. Multisensory perception is your ability to see beyond what the five senses can detect.

Set your intention every day for the next week to find meaning for you personally in your everyday experiences. Open yourself to seeing meaning that you did not see before and recognizing your insights as valuable experiences of multisensory perception. Take notes and journal every night about what you have seen from your multisensory perception.

At the end of the week write down your answers to these questions:

- *What was your most meaningful example of multisensory perception? What did you learn from this experience?*
- *How did your intention to find meaning in your everyday life affect your experiences? Be specific.*
- *How did what you discovered affect your perspective of yourself and others? Give examples.*

Now take another week and set the same intention every day. Take notes and journal every night about what you have seen from your multisensory perspective.

At the end of this time write your answers to these questions:

- *What did you discover about yourself by opening to your multisensory perception? Be specific.*
- *What was the first multisensory experience in your life that you recognized as a multisensory experience?*
- *What is the most meaningful example of a multisensory experience in your life?*

Helpful Diagram

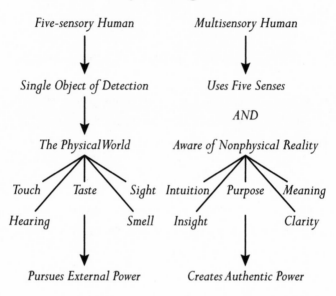

— Chapter 2 —

This chapter is about your intellect and your five senses. They are related. Your five senses provide your intellect information—what you see, hear, taste, touch, and smell. Your intellect compares and analyzes this information, deduces and concludes things about it, and tells you how to stay alive and comfortable. It cannot comprehend information that does not come from your five senses. That is the kind of information that multisensory perception provides you. It literally "makes no sense" to your intellect. We call this information "illogical" or "non-sense," for example, experiences of other personalities of your soul that live in different times and different places, such as the past, from the perspective of your personality. Yet it is precisely this kind of information that is now necessary for us to create healthy, empowered, and constructive lives. The intellect cannot even imagine this new circumstance. This chapter is about exactly this circumstance. In the East it is called karma, and in the West it is called the Golden Rule.

— Karma —

Creating authentic power requires that you become responsible for everything that you create. The Universal Law of Cause and Effect shows you how you already *are* responsible for everything that you create, and knowledge of it gives you a strong incentive to create healthy and constructive experiences with your choices. This is the law of karma: What you cause another to experience, you or another personality of your soul will experience also. Conversely, what another personality of your soul causes in the experience of another, you may experience also. Karma is the impersonal Universal teacher of responsibility. When you understand that your experiences are karmic necessities, you are less likely to take them personally—to react with anger, righteous outrage, judgment, etc. (Remember: Judge not lest you be judged.) This means that you also will create fewer painful experiences and more joyful experiences for yourself and other personalities of your soul. When you choose wisely and responsibly while you are angry, judgmental, etc., you enter into the evolution of your soul consciously (and you create authentic power).

If you are reading an eBook, click the following link to go to an expanded online version of this Chapter Study Guide, including video, meditation, and support for study groups. If you are reading a print copy, type it into your browser: www.seatofthesoul.com/sg2.

Questions

Here are more questions to ask yourself. If you feel reactions to any of them (such as becoming judgmental, dismissive, appreciative, amazed, validated), make a note of these reactions. If you are in a group, share your answers and listen with openness to the experiences of fellow souls who share with you. Write your answers down so that you will remember them. You may discover that some of them change over time.

1. *How many times this last week did you feel angry, resentful, betrayed, superior, inferior, etc., and acted on that emotion?*
2. *Have you ever asked yourself, Why me? What did I do to deserve this? Write down some examples.*
3. *How many times have you felt hurt and wanted to hurt the person you felt was responsible?*
4. *Would you have acted the same way if you knew that the cause of your hurt may have occurred centuries before you were born?*
5. *How do you feel about the possibility of consciously creating blissful experiences for yourself and for other personalities of your soul? Imagine how you could do this. Write all that comes to you and go back to it frequently. Choose what experiences you intend to bring into your life.*

Exercises

A Week of Kindness

Go out of your way to see how you can be friendly and kind to people that you encounter during this week. Extend this kindness to people you talk to on the phone, email, or write. Then notice how you feel and what effects you notice in your life. Share your experiences with others, and if they are not also doing this exercise, invite them to join you and to share their experiences as you share yours.

(From *The Mind of the Soul* by Gary Zukav and Linda Francis)

Exploring the Golden Rule

Remember a time when something happened to you that you were surprised and delighted about, for example, an unexpected gift or kindness.

Ask yourself, "Have I ever surprised and delighted others in a similar way?"

Remember when something happened and you were shocked and hurt, for example, when you were betrayed or someone raged at you.

Ask yourself, "Have I ever shocked and hurt others in a similar way?"

Have you ever considered that the things you are experiencing, joyful or painful, are consequences of choices you have made or that another personality of your soul has made?

Pondering these questions will stimulate deeper connections and conversations with the people in your life.

(From *The Mind of the Soul* by Gary Zukav and Linda Francis)

A Karmic Experience?

Recall a time when you were aware that you were or might be having a karmic experience . . . an experience that you felt or sensed had to do with karma that you created or that had been created by another personality of your soul. How did it impact your life? It may be that you sensed that there was more to this experience . . . more happening than you could articulate.

Explore this by yourself and/or with others. Ask your intuition how knowing this can support you in your spiritual growth.

If you have not had such an experience, imagine what one would feel like to you.

Chapter 3 ──

In the past, reverence meant putting something, such as Divinity, or someone, such as a saint, above and beyond human experience. Now we can sense ourselves and others in ways that we cannot detect with our eyes, ears, nose, taste, and touch. We do not confuse the things that our five senses tell us about a person, such as her sex, skin color, or nationality, with her essence. Five-sensory humans do not mistake the clothes that an individual is wearing—for example, a business suit, evening gown, or work jeans—with the individual that is wearing them. In the same way, multisensory humans do not mistake an Earth suit, such as a white, American artist or a yellow, Thai nun or a black, African teacher with the soul that is wearing it. Multisensory humans also sense oceans, forests, deserts, and mountains in ways that five-sensory humans cannot. Connecting with the essence of a person or thing is a multisensory experience. This is reverence. Reverence is different from respect. You can respect one person without respecting another person, but you cannot revere one person without revering everyone.

— Reverence —

Reverence is seeing beyond the outer shell of appearance to the essence within it. Reverence is connecting with the true power and essence of what a person is or what a thing is. It is a holy perception. It is recognizing personalities as Earth suits and shifting your attention away from the Earth suit to what is wearing it. That is the soul. Reverence is accepting that all Life is, in and of itself, sacred. Without reverence we become cruel and destructive and create painful karma for ourselves. A reverent person automatically avoids the severe karmic consequences that are created by acting without reverence, and each reverent action is a step toward aligning itself with its soul. The soul reveres all of Life. A reverent person sees and honors Divinity in all its forms. Living with reverence requires challenging the values and perceptions of a five-sensory world that does not value Life. Becoming reverent is essentially becoming a spiritual person.

If you are reading an eBook, click the following link to go to an expanded online version of this Chapter Study Guide, including video, meditation, and support for study groups. If you are reading a print copy, type it into your browser: www.seatofthesoul.com/sg3.

Questions

Use these questions to bring your attention to experiences of reverence. Allow them to stimulate new perceptions and insights in you.

1. *How often do you judge the people around you because of their skin color, appearance, clothing, beliefs, actions, and possessions? (Sometimes this question is difficult to answer because the parts of your personality that judge others are so familiar to you that their judgments don't seem like judgments. They seem like the way things actually are. So take at least a day to observe how often you judge others or yourself and write down your judgments as you notice them.)*

2. *Do you notice when you think people are judging you for the same reasons? Write and/or share your observations.*

3. *Can people earn your reverence, like they can earn your respect? Notice what you feel when you feel reverence and what you feel when you have respect for others. Write what you notice and share it with others, if possible.*

4. *Do you see Divinity in* all *forms of Life?*

5. *Would you like to? Spend a day or two seeing if you can sense Divinity wherever you look.*

Exercise

Can You See Differently?

(If you are with others, one person read this exercise while the others close their eyes.)

- *Recall a person whom you have known for a long time but you don't feel close to and you would like to. Do you feel inferior to or jealous of your friend? Or perhaps superior and judgmental? Why do you feel distant from this person?*
- *Have you been looking only at your friend's Earth suit?*
- *Have you been focusing on what he does or how he dresses?*
- *Do you feel you are not able to communicate because of a misunderstanding or a fight you had?*
- *Are you distant because your life has taken you in a different direction?*

Now open yourself to the possibility of seeing your friend differently. Set your intention to see beyond the appearances of your friend's Earth suit. Spend at least fifteen minutes on this exercise.

Picture your friend. Remind yourself that you don't know all that goes into the life of your friend . . . his challenges, his fears, his joys, his terror.

Remember that you are a soul and so is your friend.

If your eyes were closed, open them and notice how you feel about your friend now. Do you feel compassion? If not, continue to do this exercise over and over until you feel a shift from contraction to openness, from seeing your friend only as a personality to knowing that your friend is a soul wearing an Earth suit. Allow yourself to feel the instant that your fear, judgment, and disdain disappear and reverence appears. Do this daily for as long as you like and choose different people in your life that you would like to change your perspective on from judgmental to reverent.

(From *The Mind of the Soul* by Gary Zukav and Linda Francis)

Life Lesson

Set the intention this week to see with reverence everyone and everything, including your relationships with people who are close to you, acquaintances, people you meet in passing, people you feel a distance from, etc. Set this intention each morning and every time you remember during the day.

At the end of the week write your answers to these questions:

- *What did looking at everything with reverence during the last week help you to realize? Give examples.*
- *What did you create by holding this intention? Be specific.*

Exercises and Questions

Use these questions to help you explore reverence:

1   *Your soul reveres Life in all of its forms, including you. Do you revere you?*

2. *What would it mean to revere yourself?*

3. *Would revering yourself be narcissistic? Some fear-based parts of your personality may feel narcissistic. It is important to become aware of them so that you can tell the difference between narcissism and revering yourself. Write and/or share about your discoveries.*

4. *What would it mean to revere someone else?*

5. *If reverence is recognizing the essence of a person or thing, how could you revere the essence of someone else and not revere your essence?*

6. *If you revered all things, how would your life be different?*

— Chapter 4 —

Your emotions are very important. You cannot grow spiritually without becoming aware of them. This turns the view of emotions that most of us hold upside down. We think that emotions serve no useful purpose. Like an appendix, they can be very painful, and nothing is lost by having an appendix removed. A wonderful treasure is lost when you are removed from your emotions. Your emotions are messages from your soul that bring you priceless information. If you do not receive the information, it is delivered again and again. Not only pleasing and blissful emotions bring you important information. Painful emotions, including the most unbearable, bring you important information, too. In other words, the path to spiritual growth leads through your heart.

Only through your emotions can you experience the force field of your own soul. Your emotions tell you what parts of your personality are loving and create joyful consequences when you act on them and what parts are fearful and create painful consequences when you act on them. As you become spiritual, you become heart-centered. Many people feel that "heart-centered" means mushy and sentimental, but that is actually the opposite of heart-centered. Becoming heart-centered means choosing to act from loving parts of your personality instead of frightened parts of your personality. In other words, moving from being unconsciously controlled by fearful emotions to consciously choosing to act on loved-based emotions. Once you can do this, you are in a position to change your life, your future, and your world.

—— Heart ——

The logics that enabled us to evolve as a five-sensory species cannot meaningfully represent the existence of the soul, evolution without time, or the nonphysical dynamic of karma that generates and links many lifetimes. Therefore, the time has come for a higher order of logic and understanding. The creation of this higher order of logic and understanding requires close attention to feelings, and this requires the heart. Your emotions show you which parts of your personality are aligned with your soul and which parts are not. Without awareness of your emotions, you cannot see the dynamics that lie behind your emotions or the ends that these dynamics serve. Only a compassionate heart can engage evil directly. Evil is an absence of Light, Divinity, Divine Intelligence. The remedy for an absence is a presence. Only the heart can bring Light where there was none. Therefore, only the heart can engage evil directly. Understanding evil as the absence of Light enables you to see that the only place to begin the process of eliminating evil is within yourself.

If you are reading an eBook, click the following link to go to an expanded online version of this Chapter Study Guide, including video, meditation, and support for study groups. If you are reading a print copy, type it into your browser: www.seatofthesoul.com/sg4.

Questions

Becoming aware of your emotions and using them to create authentic power does not mean ceasing to use your intellect. On the contrary, you use it more and more consciously, which means more and more in the service of the heart—in the service of love—instead of unconsciously in the service of fear.

1. *Have you ever thought of your emotions as serving a purpose beyond fight or flight survival? What emotions do you encounter in yourself that you feel are based in fear? What emotions do you experience in yourself that you feel come from love?*

2. *What does the "higher order of logic and understanding of the heart" mean to you? Write down your thoughts so that you can refer to them later.*

3. *Have you ever considered evil as an absence of love? What would this mean for you if it were true? Write about this and share from your heart with others who are open.*

4. *Have you ever considered the idea that the place to begin eliminating evil in the world is within you? Write the ideas and insights that come to you as you ponder this idea. If it were true, in what ways would you eliminate evil in you?*

Exercises

Choose Your Intentions with Your Heart

For the next day or the next week, ask yourself, "Why do I really want to do or say this?" before you choose what you do or say.

- *Is it to create harmony?*
- *Am I doing or saying what feels good in my heart?*
- *Am I doing or saying what my mind is telling me?*

Write your answers in your journal.

Once you have done this for yourself, ask others to join you in this exercise and share about it.

(From *The Mind of the Soul* by Gary Zukav and Linda Francis)

Open Your Heart

Practice opening your heart by thinking of a time when you felt love and openness for someone—for your child, grandchild, partner, friend, or in a special encounter with a stranger. Recall the situation and what you were feeling in the area of your heart.

The next time you feel your heart is closed (your chest hurts), let yourself experience the pain in your chest, breathe deeply, even if you feel constriction, and, at the same time, remember that special time. Keep opening your heart and breathing deeply until you feel yourself begin to relax, even if only a little. Ask your intuition for guidance in opening your heart.

Do this practice to challenge the fear-based part of your personality that is closing your heart to yourself and others.

(From *The Heart of the Soul* by Gary Zukav and Linda Francis)

Helpful Thought

When an intention comes from your heart, it brings the energy of your heart into your action and creates experiences for you. When your intention is not from your heart, it brings fear into your action and creates your experiences. You must be aware of what you are feeling and thinking in order to recognize the differences. Your heart is open, accepting, creative, and grounded. It feels good and relaxes you. Fear is impatient, righteous, closed, and defensive. It hurts and cannot tolerate differences. Your heart includes. Fear excludes. Your heart keeps you in touch with the whole. The whole is Life. Without your heart to illuminate your travels, they become frightening experiences.

Here is a mini-checklist to use to remind you if your heart is open or closed:

CLOSED HEART	OPEN HEART
Sentimental	Clear and Grounded
Exclusive	Inclusive

Chapter 5

It is as easy to call upon intuition as it is to ask yourself a question. In particular, questions such as "Why am I so upset about this situation?", "Why does this interaction affect me in this way?", and "What can I learn about myself from this experience?" always invoke guidance, and guidance always comes. How does this happen? Your intellect and five senses cannot explain intuition or show it to you, but you can experience intuition for yourself. It is your source of insights that help you stay in the Earth school, express your creativity, and inspire you. It allows you to benefit from compassion and wisdom that are greater than we can give to others and receive from others. Intuition is the fountain of personal truths and impersonal truths. It is natural for us to want to access intuition and enjoy it. Five-sensory humans do not think intuition is worthy of serious study. Sometimes multisensory humans think they are superior because they have intuitive abilities and so they use intuition with a closed heart. However, multisensory humans who are creating authentic power depend upon it. For them, intuition is the primary decision-making faculty.

— Intuition —

Intuition is perception beyond the physical senses that is meant to assist you. It is what makes multisensory perception multisensory. Multisensory humans are in conscious communication with advanced intelligences. They have access to compassionate and impersonal help. Multisensory humans see insights, intuitions, hunches, and inspirations as promptings from, and links to, a perspective of greater comprehension and compassion than their own. They use this guidance to help them create authentic power. Your higher self is the aspect of your soul within you. Communicating with your soul through your higher self produces personal truth—truth that mostly is effective only for you. This is an in-house intuitive process. Communicating through your higher self with souls in advance of your own soul produces impersonal truth—truth that is true for anyone who comes into contact with it. This is receiving information through intuitive channels. Multisensory personalities rely upon truths they receive from their higher selves and, through their higher selves, from their own souls and souls that are more advanced than their own.

If you are reading an eBook, click the following link to go to an expanded online version of this Chapter Study

Guide, including video, meditation, and support for study groups. If you are reading a print copy, type it into your browser: www.seatofthesoul.com/sg5.

Questions

Go back into your memory or into your creativity to find answers to these questions. If you are in a group, share your answers with your spiritual partners and open to learning about yourself from what they share with you.

1. *Have you ever had sudden or surprising insights? Have you acted on these insights? What significant things happened because you acted, or if you didn't act, what do you feel prevented you?*
2. *Have you ever been suddenly inspired by an idea, project, or possibility that was very meaningful to you, or became very meaningful?*
3. *Have you ever found yourself feeling compassion for someone who wronged you or others, even though you still do not like or approve of what he or she did?*
4. *Have you ever had the thought that you have assistance or help that you cannot see, but that you can feel is present with you?*
5. *Do the ideas that you are not alone and that you can access loving guidance through your intuition appeal to you?*

Exercise

A Daily Practice for Consulting Intuition

Anytime you react to *anything* . . .

- *I feel overwhelmed (too busy, don't have enough time, etc.)*
- *I am sad (depressed, manic, impatient, etc.)*
- *I lost my job (hate my boss, etc.)*
- *He or she disappointed me (betrayed me, cheated on me, etc.)*
- *I feel inferior (invisible, unworthy, etc.)*
- *I am upset because my car broke down (flight got canceled, etc.)*
- *I feel entitled (superior, better than, etc.)*

Ask yourself:

What can I learn about myself from this reaction?
How can I move beyond the control of this part of my personality that is reacting now?
How can I change my perspective from frightened to loving?

Listen for the answer.
It will come.

Life Lesson

Each morning this week set your intention to open to the support of intuition, support that is always there for you. Ask yourself questions that you want support with. Then listen for answers. They may come immediately or they may come later, but they will come.

Some examples of questions you might ask are:

- *How can I relate better with my son or daughter?*
- *How can I become aware of frightened parts of my personality sooner?*
- *How can I take responsibility sooner when I realize that I am in a power struggle?*
- *How can I best complete the project that I am confused about?*
- *How can I heal the frightened part of the personality that feels financially inadequate?*
- *What is the best way that I can speak with my mother-in-law (child, spouse, boss, boyfriend, neighbor, etc.)?*
- *What can I learn from my experiences of overwhelm, anger, jealousy, overeating, etc.?*

Write your questions down. Ponder them. Open yourself to answers. Notice the ways that intuitive understanding, or insight, comes to you, and open yourself to other ways as well. Listen to what you are saying when you speak and to what others are saying. Remember your dreams and meditate on them.

At the end of the week write down your answers to these questions:

- *Do you feel that this Life Lesson helped you to further develop your ability to use intuition? If so, share how. If not, ask your intuition how you can develop your ability to use intuition. Be patient. Your answer will come.*
- *What questions did you ask your intuition? What answers did you get? How did that support you?*
- *Write down the most significant thing you learned about yourself and your intuitive ability this week.*
- *Share this with someone who wants to open to their own intuitive guidance.*

Life Lesson

Devote two days this week to following your intuition. If you cannot spend the whole day, find periods of time during a day or several days. Schedule it (make appointments between you and your intuition).

Write your experiences throughout the day, and at the end of the day answer these questions in your journal:

- *When did you follow your intuition? When did you resist? Be specific.*
- *Did your intuition surprise you?*
- *What did you discover about yourself by following your intuition?*
- *What were the most significant things you experienced experimenting with your intuition?*

___ Chapter 6 ___

Most people think of themselves and others as made of "stuff," such as muscles, neurons, organs, a brain, hands, and feet. This thought is a product of five-sensory perception, which can detect only what we can see, hear, touch, taste, and smell. The perception of our species is expanding from one range of frequencies in the spectrum of nonphysical Light into another range of higher frequencies. This is the emergence of multisensory perception. As we become multisensory, we are discovering that we and everything else are made of Light. Light, Consciousness, Love, Life, and Divine Intelligence are all words for the same thing, and we are that. Most of you exists in nonphysical reality, and therefore most of your interactions occur in nonphysical reality. Your influence extends far beyond the domain of the five senses, and it is instantaneous. Consequences of choices that you make and the emotions that you feel affect others wherever they are. Energies that emanate from your personality—its fears—follow the path of physical light. They are not instantaneous. The unconditional Love of your soul is instantaneous, Universal, not bound. As you align your personality with your soul, you bring the unconditional Love of your soul into the Earth school.

— Light —

You are a system of Light. The frequency of your Light depends upon your consciousness. When you shift your consciousness, you shift the frequency of your Light. Emotions are currents of energy with different frequencies. Thoughts such as vengeance, violence, greed, and using others create low-frequency currents of energy, such as anger, hatred, jealousy, and fear. Loving, creative, and caring thoughts create high-frequency currents of energy, such as appreciation, forgiveness, and gratitude. Your choice of thoughts determines which emotional currents you will reinforce or release. Changing your thoughts changes the quality of your Light, the nature of your experiences, and your effects on others. We are evolving into a higher range of frequencies of Light, which means that we are becoming multisensory. We are becoming aware of the Light of our souls and able to communicate with forms of Life that were invisible to us, such as nonphysical Teachers. Nonphysical Teachers assist your soul in every phase of its evolution, but they cannot make your decisions for you or change your karma.

If you are reading an eBook, click the following link to go to an expanded online version of this Chapter Study

Guide, including video, meditation, and support for study groups. If you are reading a print copy, type it into your browser: www.seatofthesoul.com/sg6.

Questions

Ask yourself questions that increase your awareness of different experiences in your body and the consequences of acting on them. The energy of fear is painful in your body. This is the experience of lower-frequency currents of energy. Acting on them creates destructive consequences. The energy of Love feels wonderful in your body. This is the experience of higher-frequency currents of energy. Acting on them creates constructive consequences.

1. *Does your body feel good or painful when you are angry, or jealous, or vengeful?*
2. *What kinds of consequences have you created by acting on these emotions?*
3. *Does your body feel good or painful when you are grateful, appreciative, or content?*
4. *What kinds of consequences have you created by acting on these emotions?*
5. *Which kinds of consequences do you prefer?*

Exercise

Every Emotion Is a Message

If you are studying with someone, read this exercise to your partner or partners. If you are studying alone, read this exercise and then go through it as well as you can. You may be surprised by how much and how accurately you remember it.

Recall a time when you felt a strong emotion, such as anger, jealousy, or resentment. Close your eyes and go back to that time.

Take a few minutes to feel what this emotion felt like then and still feels like now in your body. Where did/do you feel the physical sensations of it? For example, in your chest, stomach, pelvis, neck, throat?

Recall the thoughts you were having when you experienced this emotion. For example, if you were angry, were you blaming yourself or someone else, or a situation?

How did you behave?

Recall what you said when you experienced this emotion. For example, if you were resentful, did you say something hurtful?

What would you have done differently?

What can you learn about yourself from this experience now that you were not able to learn at the time?

My friend Maya Angelou says, "When you know better, you do better."

Helpful Thoughts

My emotions come from my energy-processing system
Not
From my interactions with people or things.
Each emotion is a message for me.
It is a message from my soul.
I ignore these messages when I
Act them out
By
Blaming myself, others, or the Universe.
If I do not accept these messages
They come back until I do.

Exercise

Your Spiritual Tutor

Imagine that your emotions are being sent to you by your spiritual tutor. Those that come with painful physical sensations are showing you what lower-frequency currents of light feel like in your body so that you can avoid creating destructive consequences for yourself by acting on them. Those that come with good-feeling physical sensations are showing you what higher-frequency currents of light feel like in your body so that you can create constructive consequences for yourself by acting on them. Practice listening to your spiritual tutor throughout the day. Write what you discover.

Share with others who want to practice with you.

— Chapter 7 —

Have you ever considered that the creation of your experiences is governed by the law of cause and effect? The physical law of cause and effect governs physical causes and physical effects, such as launching a rocket and landing it on the moon. The Universal Law of Cause and Effect governs the creation of physical and nonphysical effects by *nonphysical* causes. If you are not aware of the Universal Law of Cause and Effect and how it works, you will create, as you continually do, but you will not create what you want. Your intentions are the nonphysical causes that create your experiences. This is one of the most important things in your life to remember. You can experiment to see if it is true. Experimenting with your life frees you to create differently. It requires becoming aware moment to moment of your intentions and then looking for connections between them and the experiences that you encounter. The more aware you become of your intentions, and the more aware you become of your experiences, the more connections you will see between them, and the more you will be able to consciously choose the experiences of your life that you want. This is the development of mastery. It is the creation of authentic power.

— Intention I —

There is Light, and there is the shaping of Light by consciousness. This is creation. You are a dynamic being of Light that informs the Light flowing through you with each intention. An intention is the reason for acting. It is the use of your will. Intentions set into motion processes that affect every aspect of your life. Physical reality and everything in it are systems of Light within systems of Light, and this Light is the same Light as the Light of your soul. Physical matter is the densest level of Light. We are evolving into a species of individuals who are aware of themselves as beings of Light and shape their Light consciously with wisdom and compassion. You create your reality with your intentions. It is a multilayered creation—personal, family, work/school, people in your life, town/city, state/area, culture, nation, race, sex, soul of humanity. No individuals have the same reality. As you move outward through the layers of your reality, they become increasingly impersonal. The shared physical reality of the Earth school is a fluid massive consciousness in which each individual exists independently and also coexists interdependently with others.

If you are reading an eBook, click the following link to go to an expanded online version of this Chapter Study Guide, including video, meditation, and support for study groups. If you are reading a print copy, type it into your browser: www.seatofthesoul.com/sg7.

Questions

1. *What is the difference between a desire and an intention?*
2. *Are you generally aware of your intentions?*
3. *If you knew that your intentions create your reality, would you pay more attention to them?*
4. *Can you think of anyone except you who can know your intention at the moment that you speak or act?*
5. *How does the idea that you and every physical form are the same Light as the Light of your soul make you feel?*

Exercises

The Fundamental Practice

Before you do anything that you are not sure of your motivation for doing, ask yourself:

"What is my intention for doing this?"

And wait for an answer.

Do this for several days and see how your experiences change. Write what you discover. Do this as a practice daily if you find it is supporting you.

(From *The Mind of the Soul* by Gary Zukav and Linda Francis)

Life Lessons

For the next week or more, ask yourself, "What is my intention?" every time you react. For example, if you are impatient, defensive, angry, or in a power struggle, *stop* and ask yourself in that moment, "What is my intention?" Not the intention you think you have set for yourself, but the real intention that lies behind your impatience, defensiveness, anger, or the power struggle.

Feel the physical sensations in your body in the vicinities of your energy-processing centers and, while you are feeling them, decide what you will say or do next. Ask yourself, "What would be the healthiest choice for me right now?"

Carry a notebook in your purse or pocket and write your discoveries.

If you are studying with a group, share with your spiritual partners what you are learning about intention or questions you have about it.

After the first week, write your answers to these questions in your journal:

- *What have you discovered so far?*
- *What were some of the healthy choices you made instead of acting from a frightened part of your personality?*
- *What did you discover about your intentions when you were in a reaction and you stopped to ask, "What is my intention?" Give some specific examples.*

- *What was your most common way to react? In other words, what frightened part of your personality became active most frequently?*
- *If you are studying with others, what did you learn from sharing with your spiritual partners?*

During the second week consider the choices you have made so far and see if you can distinguish between your surface intention or intentions (for example, a physical goal) and your deeper intention (why you are going to do what you are going to do). Don't forget to continue to ask yourself, "What is my intention?" each time you are about to react, and then, ask yourself instead, "What would be the healthiest choice for me right now?"

If you are in a group, continue to share what you are learning about intention or your questions about it.

After the second week write your answers to these questions in your journal:

- *Were you able to distinguish between your surface intention or intentions and your deepest, bedrock intentions? Give examples.*
- *What was the most significant thing you discovered this week about intentions and yourself?*
- *What did you learn about your intentions from your interactions with others?*

— Chapter 8 —

Your choice of intention creates your experiences. When you encounter the experiences that your choice has created, you must again choose an intention. This process continues until your soul leaves the Earth school. While you choose the same intentions, you create the same consequences. This is called karma in the East and the Golden Rule in the West. When you choose different intentions, you create different karma. By choosing intentions that come from love instead of intentions that come from fear, you create joyful karma instead of painful karma. Karma teaches you responsibility for the intentions that you choose, and you learn this lesson at your own pace. How long will you continue to create painful experiences for yourself? That depends on how long you continue to choose intentions of fear. The choice is yours, and the intention behind each of your choices creates more experiences for you. Each word that you speak carries intelligence, and therefore is an intention that shapes Light. When you choose to align yourself with your soul instead of with your personality, you create a reality that reflects your soul rather than your personality. You create "heaven on Earth" when you choose to respond to life's difficulties with intentions of love instead of intentions of fear.

—— Intention II ——

What is not learned in a lifetime is carried over into other lifetimes along with new lessons that arise for the soul to learn. This is how the soul evolves. The karma of the soul determines the characteristics of the personality at birth, including its intentions. There are two fundamental intentions: love and fear. The intentions of the personality at birth shape the Light that is flowing through it into the reality that is optimal for the evolution of its soul. The reactions of the personality to the consequences of its intentions become additional karma for the soul. This continues until its intentions are changed. That requires consciousness. The introduction of consciousness into the cyclic process of creation allows you to change your intentions from fear to love, change your karma, and infuse physical matter with the consciousness of the sacred. Spiritual partnership is partnership between equals for the purpose of creating authentic power. Spiritual partners are aware of their souls, and they are committed to bringing the consciousness of their souls into their intention-setting processes and assisting one another in doing that.

If you are reading an eBook, click the following link

to go to an expanded online version of this Chapter Study Guide, including video, meditation, and support for study groups. If you are reading a print copy, type it into your browser: www.seatofthesoul.com/sg8.

Questions

Are these questions new to you? What is new about them? What is most useful to you about them?

1. *Have you ever considered the karma you create with your intentions to be your* soul's *karma?*

2. *Have you ever thought about your experiences as the balancing of your soul's energy?*

3. *If the experiences of your life really were karmic necessities, would you allow frightened parts of your personality to react to them (and create destructive, painful karma)?*

4. *What kind of karma do you want to create for yourself—blissful or painful?*

5. *What would you need to change about yourself in order to do that?*

Helpful Thought

A Tree by Its Fruits

You can always identify a tree by its fruit.
In the same way, you can always identify
your intentions by your experiences.

(From *The Heart of the Soul* by Gary Zukav and Linda Francis)

Who Are You Attracting?

Take a moment to think about the people in your life. In general, are they people who:

- *Please others so they feel better themselves?*
- *Gossip?*
- *Love life?*
- *Trust the Universe?*
- *Don't understand why things happen to them?*
- *Want revenge?*
- *Are angry and don't shout?*
- *Give freely?*

Life Lesson

This Life Lesson is about hidden agendas—what they are, how to recognize them, and what they can tell you about yourself. Discovering agendas that you are not aware of is the same as discovering frightened parts of your personality. You think that your intention is one thing, but a frightened part of your personality has another intention. That is your hidden agenda, and it will remain hidden from you as long as you are unaware of the frightened part of your personality that holds it.

A hidden agenda may be trying to impress someone, dominate someone, feel better about yourself by teaching him, etc. For example, you might think that your intention is to help someone understand authentic power and not recognize that you feel superior while you are in a teaching role.

This week set your intention to uncover any hidden agendas you may have.

When you discover during your interactions with others that you have a hidden agenda, celebrate your discovery, even though it means that you will experience painful physical sensations. They are not enjoyable, but identifying frightened parts of your personality and not being controlled by them is. For example, it can be exhilarating to fully feel a need to withdraw, defend yourself, or become angry and not be controlled by it at the same time.

At the end of the week, write down your answers to these questions:

- *How did looking for hidden agendas support you this week?*
- *What hidden agendas did you discover in yourself?*
- *What was the most difficult part of this Life Lesson?*
- *What were your most significant discoveries about yourself?*

— Chapter 9 —

Multisensory personalities and five-sensory personalities that are becoming multisensory evolve through the conscious choices that they make. This is a very big change in human evolution. Unconscious evolution through experiences that are created unconsciously by unconscious intentions has been the way our species evolved until now. As you become conscious of the different parts of your personality, you become able to experience consciously the forces within you that compete for expression, that lay claim to the single intention that will be yours at each moment, that will shape your reality. Five-sensory humans do not see these choices as important. Multisensory humans recognize them as heroic. Depending on your choices, you step closer to your soul or closer to your personality. The energy of your personality is contracted, fearful, and predatory. The energy of your soul is open, joyful, and giving. Which do you choose? What more important choice can you make?

— Choice —

Choice is the engine of our evolution. Each choice is a choice of intention. An intention is a quality of consciousness that you bring to an action or thought. A responsible choice is a choice that takes into account the consequences of your choice. You must ask yourself, "Am I ready to accept all the consequences of this choice?", "Is this what I really want?" You must become aware of the different parts of your personality in order to choose responsibly. Responsible choice is the accelerated way of evolution of the multisensory personality. When you enter your decision-making dynamic consciously, you enter consciously into your own evolution. Each time you create with the intentions of the soul— forgiveness, humbleness, clarity, and love—you empower yourself. This is how authentic power is built up—step by step, choice by choice. Temptation draws your awareness to negativity in you that would create painful karma if it were allowed to remain unconscious. It enables your soul to evolve directly through conscious choice without creating negative karma. You cleanse yourself of negativity without actually having to live through the experience.

If you are reading an eBook, click the following link to go to an expanded online version of this Chapter Study Guide, including video, meditation, and support for study groups. If you are reading a print copy, type it into your browser: www.seatofthesoul.com/sg9.

Questions

These questions are not about what you know; they are about where you are in your awareness. If you are not aware of the dynamics within you that are creating your experiences, the experiences they create will always be (1) surprising ("Why me?") and (2) painful. Take a look at where you are in your awareness.

1. *Have you ever asked yourself before acting or speaking, "What will this most likely create?"*
2. *If so, have you ever followed up with the question "Is this what I really want to create—not just what I want in the moment?"*
3. *If you knew that you could change the course of your life and the evolution of your soul by asking yourself these questions each time before you act or speak, would you ask them?*
4. *Have you ever thought of temptation as a positive dynamic?*
5. *What do you think about the idea that a temptation is a dress rehearsal for a negative karmic event?*

Exercise

Choosing Anew

Think of a situation that comes up in your life frequently where you consistently behave the same way—argue with your spouse, have painful interactions with your parents or children, or are impatient with a co-worker or with things that need to be fixed or with a driver on the freeway. Think of something that you would like to change. If you are studying with another or others, take turns. One of you read this exercise and the others close your eyes. Then switch. If you are studying alone, read the exercise, then close your eyes and do it as you remember it.

Close your eyes. Recall this situation, but this time remember it as though you were watching yourself in it. Consider the possibility that you have been encountering situations of this kind in order to learn how to handle them differently, in a more conscious and constructive way.

As you relive this situation in your imagination, remember it up to the time when you did the thing that you would rather not have done. And this time, choose a more healthy response, one that will create consequences that you would much rather experience. Realize that choosing a more healthy response will require courage on your part. Now choose that healthy response. Allow yourself to see the different consequences that it creates. Write what you discovered and share with each other if you are doing this exercise with a partner or partners.

Life Lesson

For the next week, focus on making your choices consciously. Set your intention each morning and anytime you remember during the day to make responsible choices. Say to yourself, "I am responsible for the choices I make and the consequences they create," each time you are aware of making a choice. When you are unclear about what to choose, ask yourself, "What would be the healthiest choice I could make?" Creating authentic power means making the healthiest choice you can in the moment—the choice that may stretch you and will always empower you. For example, the choice not to eat something you know your body does not need; not to shout when you are angry; not to complain when you need to blame; not to gossip when you can hardly wait to talk about someone; to say no when someone asks you to do something that you know is not healthy for you to do, etc.

At the end of the week, write down your answers to these questions:

- *How did reminding yourself "I am responsible for the choices I make and the consequences they create" affect your choices?*
- *What is the most significant discovery you made about yourself this week?*

Helpful Thought

RESPONSIBILITY
is
a
SACRED
word.

It
means
the ability
to respond
from
LOVE
rather than
automatically reacting
from
FEAR.

This
is
CREATING
AUTHENTIC POWER.

— Chapter 10 —

Have you ever wondered why addictions are so difficult? Addictions are the strongest frightened parts of your personality. The greater the desire of your soul to heal your addiction, the greater will be the cost of keeping it. This is the compassionate Universe showing you that your inadequacy is so deep that only something of equal or greater value in opposition to it will stop you. Healing an addiction requires you to test your power of choice, to discover for yourself that the only intention that will empower you must come from a place within you that suggests that you are indeed able to make responsible choices and draw power from them. Each time you choose to challenge your addiction, you disengage from its power and more and more increase your personal power. You bring to light, heal, and release the deepest currents of negativity within you. As you face your deepest struggles, you reach for your highest goals. When you struggle with an addiction, you deal directly with the healing of your soul. This is the work that you were born to do.

— Addiction —

You cannot begin to heal an addiction until you acknowledge that you are addicted. Acknowledging an addiction is acknowledging that a part of you is out of control. Once an addiction has been acknowledged, it cannot be ignored, and it cannot be healed without changing your life completely. Addictions cannot be satiated. A sexual addiction cannot be satiated by sex, a food addiction by food, an alcohol addiction by alcohol. Addictions are frightened parts of your personality that are controlled completely by external circumstances. They are your greatest inadequacies. Sexual addictions are the most universal because issues of power are tied directly to the learning of sexuality. You cannot be in your power and sexually out of control simultaneously. When you challenge an addiction, you stand between your lesser self and your full self—between unconscious permission to act unconsciously and a conscious life. Each time you challenge an addiction you create authentic power and contribute directly to the evolution of your soul.

If you are reading an eBook, click the following link to go to an expanded online version of this Chapter Study Guide, including video, meditation, and support for study groups. If you are reading a print copy, type it into your browser: www.seatofthesoul.com/sg10.

Questions

Everyone has addictions. If you feel that you are an exception, experiment with approaching these questions with an open mind and an open heart.

1. *Do you know any parts of your personality that are out of your control—for example, eating, drinking, smoking, gambling, sex, watching pornography?*
2. *Has giving this part of your personality what it demands ever increased your control over it?*
3. *Do you recognize any parts of your personality that might be out of control—for example, are you certain that you can stop drinking a glass of wine with dinner, pass by a 75-percent-off sale, leave pastries out of your diet?*
4. *How does the idea that a part of your personality might be out of your control make you feel?*
5. *What do you feel are your greatest inadequacies, or would be if you were aware of them?*

Exercises

Passion or Addiction?

Make a list of your daily activities, including your leisure activities. For each activity, ask yourself the following questions and write down your answers:

- *Does it unfold in its own time or do I push it?*
- *Does it open possibilities or close them?*

- *Does it open perceptions or close them?*
- *Am I avoiding my emotions or welcoming them?*
- *Is this an unfolding of joy or an unfolding of fear?*
- *Am I only self-concerned or do I care for others and the Earth?*
- *Is this a passion or a diversion?*

(From *The Heart of the Soul* by Gary Zukav and Linda Francis)

HELPFUL INFORMATION

Unraveling a Sexual Addiction

Stage One—Denial

"I am just a loving person."
"Maybe there is something to look at."
"It's not a problem, but I'll look at it if you're upset about it."

Stage Two—Acceptance

"There is something there."
"This could be a problem"
"All right. Maybe there is a problem"
"Okay. There is a problem."
"This is a big problem."

Stage Three—Opening to Healing

"I am out of control."

(From *The Heart of the Soul* by Gary Zukav and Linda Francis)

Life Lesson

This week search inside yourself for any addictions you might have, even if you can't imagine yourself having an addiction. Remember, an addiction is a very strong frightened part of your personality, and everyone has frightened parts of their personalities. Become aware of any Story you have about this behavior. A Story is not your history. Your history is simply what happened to you. Your Story is what you tell yourself and others to explain why you are the way that you are, and why you are not going to change. For example, "I had an alcoholic father," "I was sexually abused as a child," "My parents divorced when I was young," etc.

If you do not think you have any addictions, recall a part of your personality that you notice is sometimes out of your control, such as overeating, watching TV, playing cards, drinking wine with dinner, etc.

As soon as you recognize this part of your personality, write down the Story you have been telling yourself about being the way that you are when you would rather be different, or for your life not working the way that you want. Write in terms of parts of your personality. For example, "I have a frightened part of my personality that works (reads, watches TV, fixes things, etc.) all the time" or "I have a frightened part of my personality that feels it has a right to do nothing, or that feels guilty about doing nothing, etc."

Set your intention each morning to find opportunities you have been given to create authentic power that you did not recognize in the past. Remember that whatever you discover is part of your curriculum in the Earth school, and be gentle with yourself.

At the end of the week, write down your answers to these questions:

- *What differences are you able to see between the way you told your Story at the beginning of the week and the way you see it now?*
- *Were you able to see the behavior of a frightened part of your personality that you did not previously recognize as an addiction?*
- *Were you able to recognize an addiction that you were aware of in the past but that you can now see as a frightened part of your personality? How has this affected your perception of yourself?*

Chapter 11

There are certain growing dynamics that can occur only within the dynamic of commitment. Without commitment, you cannot learn to care for another person more than yourself. The archetype of spiritual partnership is designed for the conscious journey of multisensory humans toward authentic power. This is different from the archetype of marriage, which was designed to assist physical survival, and in which the partners do not necessarily see themselves as equals. When you commit to a spiritual partnership with another human being, or other human beings, you begin to value your partners' contribution to your development and to experience their perceptions and observations as helpful and, indeed, central, to your growth, to see that conversations between you stir deep waters. You learn to trust not only one another but also your ability to grow together. You are related to every form of Life upon this planet and beyond. In other words, as you choose to participate consciously in more inclusive levels of interaction, you take on not only your own transformation but also those of the larger collectives in which you participate. Your evolution toward authentic power, therefore, affects not only you.

—— Relationships ——

Without commitment you cannot learn to see others as your soul sees them—as beautiful spirits of Light. Spiritual partnership is partnership between equals for the purpose of spiritual growth. Spiritual partners recognize the existence of the soul and consciously seek to further its evolution. They set aside the wants of their personalities in order to accommodate the needs of their partners' spiritual growth. That is how spiritual partnership works. Individuals in spiritual partnership at the level of organization, city, nation, race, and sex create new values and behaviors at these levels. The choice is always between lower-frequency energies of the personality (fear and doubt) and higher-frequency energies of the soul (love and trust). The external power that separates nations is the same that separates individuals. Individuals who align themselves with their souls will bring sexes, races, nations, and neighbors into harmony. It is not just you that is evolving through your decisions but the entirety of humanity. What is in one is in the whole, and, therefore, each of us is ultimately responsible for the whole world.

If you are reading an eBook, click the following link to go to an expanded online version of this Chapter Study

Guide, including video, meditation, and support for study groups. If you are reading a print copy, type it into your browser: www.seatofthesoul.com/sg11.

Questions

Think about how different spiritual partnerships are from every other form of relationship. Because you are reading this book, you may already be experimenting with spiritual partnerships without even thinking in these terms, or are attracted to them. Use these questions to look at yourself as a potential spiritual partner:

1. *What especially resonates with you about being a spiritual partner?*
2. *What about the idea of being a spiritual partner feels difficult to you?*
3. *What does it feel like to you to feel equal with others? If you cannot think of an experience of feeling equal (this is common), imagine what it would feel like.*
4. *How do you think the world would be different if everyone thought in terms of choosing between love and fear with each choice?*
5. *How would your world be different if you thought in terms of choosing between love and fear with each choice?*

Exercise

Doing It Differently

Do the opposite of what you usually do when you are in a power struggle. Which role do you usually play in a particular relationship, superior or inferior? If you are studying in a group, and/or if your partner is willing, role-play the opposite way (if you are usually inferior, role-play being superior, etc.). Imagine that you have been in this power struggle many times before (which you have), but this time you are going to change what you usually do. If you usually yell, you are going to withdraw. If you usually withdraw, you are going to get defensive and argumentative.

――――― ―――――

Now imagine that you are going to have the same power struggle, but this time you are going to practice using the Authentic Power Guidelines. Using the Authentic Power Guidelines (download them from www.seatofthesoul.com), role-play with your partner how you would interact differently in a power struggle. Imagine how you would handle the power struggle in yourself and act and speak from the healthiest parts of you that you can in the moment.

Write some notes in your journal to remind you to be aware when you enter a power struggle (or react in any way). These will help you remember to respond instead of react when a fear-based part of your personality becomes activated.

Life Lesson

Open yourself to cultivating loving parts of your personality. Every day this week, set your intention to do everything you can to choose love with every person you encounter. During your interactions take notes about your experiences; notice when loving parts of your personality are active and when frightened parts are active.

If you had difficulty experiencing equality, be gentle with yourself. Set your intention again to cultivate the loving parts of your personality (they always feel equal with others) and challenge the frightened parts of your personality (they always feel superior or inferior).

At the end of the week, write your answers to these questions. If you are studying with a group, share them.

- *What were two instances when you consciously chose to create with a loving part of your personality and experienced equality with others?*
  - *What thoughts and intentions were you having?*
  - *What physical sensations were you having?*
- *Write at least one specific consequence that occurred as a result of your choice to create with a loving part of the personality.*
- *What have you learned about yourself from this Life Lesson?*

Exercise

Potential Spiritual Partner

Pick someone you would like to have a deeper and more substantive relationship with, for example, a friend, sibling, spouse, or co-worker from whom you would be willing to receive feedback about yourself. Now pick a frightened part of your personality that you want to focus on—one that you don't always notice until after you have acted on it (for example, a part of your personality that is angry and shouts, or feels superior and acts entitled, or feels inferior and tries to please others). Make sure this is a part of your personality that you would like help in seeing when it becomes active so that you can challenge it before it creates painful consequences for you again. Now ask the person you chose to tell you when he or she thinks that part of your personality is active.

Write all your interactions in your journal and also write what you learned about yourself from each one.

— Chapter 12 —

Awareness of our souls lies at the heart of creating authentic power and the need to create authentic power. Since our origin as a species we have experienced ourselves as personalities—time-bound between birth and death, fearful and limited. Religions speak of souls, but few practioners act as though they have a soul. Multisensory perception is changing all this. The choice between personality/fear and soul/love is now the pivot point of our evolution, and you must choose to align yourself with your soul again and again in order to evolve. Each choice that you make brings you closer to the Earth and your personality or to your soul and its unfathomable love. Human evolution now requires us to take the health and evolution of our souls into account. This is new. Entirely new.

— Souls —

Your soul is the essence of who you are. It is the powerful, expansive, evolving center of all that you are. As we become multisensory, we become able for the first time to consider our souls in real and practical ways, to relate them to our experiences and investigate how we can use knowledge of our souls to create the most constructive lives that we can and assist our souls on their evolutionary journeys. The idea of a soul as a static, perfect entity is a sterile attempt to understand it as an "ideal form," as Plato put it. The Universe and everything in it evolves toward greater awareness and freedom. Your soul is of the Universe, or Divine Intelligence. Divine Intelligence takes on individual forms, droplets, massively reducing its power to small particles of individual consciousness. The power in each particle is as full, immortal, creative, and expressive as it is in the whole, but its energy is reduced appropriately to its form. As that little form grows in power and selfhood, it becomes larger and more Divine. Then it becomes Divine Intelligence. Your soul is such a particle.

This process parallels the process of your personality, which is of your soul, expanding into your higher self, the full power of your soul incarnate. It also parallels the process of your personality and higher self reentering the fullness of your soul when you leave the Earth. You cannot appreciate the immensity of what you are and the processes in which you are participating without taking into account your soul.

If you are reading an eBook, click the following link to go to an expanded online version of this Chapter Study Guide, including video, meditation, and support for study groups. If you are reading a print copy, type it into your browser: www.seatofthesoul.com/sg12.

Questions

Spend some time with these questions and write down the thoughts that come to you. Come back to them often, and notice if your answers change.

1. *Have you ever really thought about the soul? About your soul?*
2. *Consider: If I have a soul, what is my soul?*
3. *Ask yourself, What does my soul want?*
4. *Then ask yourself, What is the relationship between my soul and me?*
5. *Then ask yourself, How does my soul affect my life?*

Helpful Thought

The Purpose of the Earth School

The purpose of the Earth school
is to assist you in learning
how to create
AUTHENTIC POWER.
To inhabit the Earth with the
Perceptions
Values
and
Goals
of your soul.
They are
HARMONY
COOPERATION
SHARING
REVERENCE FOR LIFE.

Exercises

See What Happens

Pick an intention of the soul—harmony, cooperation, sharing, or reverence for Life—that you feel you need most in your life. For the next thirty days set this intention each morning. Each night review your day and notice when you chose it with your words and actions and when you did not. What happened when you chose it? What happened when you did not?

(From *The Mind of the Soul* by Gary Zukav and Linda Francis)

Seeing Differently

Think of a person you have known for a long time but you don't feel close to and you would like to. Do you feel inferior to or jealous of this person? Or perhaps superior and judgmental? Why do you feel distant from this person?

Have you been looking only at his or her Earth suit?
Have you been focusing on her deeds or how he dresses?
Have you had a misunderstanding or a fight?
Have your lives taken you in different directions?

Open to the possibility of seeing this person differently. Then close your eyes and picture this person. Set your intention to see beyond the appearances of her or his Earth suit.

Remind yourself that you don't know all that goes into his or her life—challenges and fears, joys and terror. Remember that you are a soul, and so is this person.

Notice how you feel about this person now. Do you feel compassion? If not, do this exercise over and over until you feel a shift from contraction to openness, from seeing this person only as a personality to knowing that he or she is a soul wearing an Earth suit. Allow yourself to feel the instant that your fear, judgment, and disdain disappear and reverence appears.

(From *The Mind of the Soul* by Gary Zukav and Linda Francis)

A True Story

My adopted Sioux brother, Phil Lane, Jr., told me this story. A female elder once asked him, "Nephew, what is the holiest of all ceremonies?" My Sioux brother thought carefully and then answered, "Vision quest, sweat lodge, or sun dance." "Yes," said the old woman, "those are all holy and sacred ceremonies, but the holiest of all ceremonies is the birth of a child." Then she looked directly at him and asked, "Then what does that make you?"

— Chapter 13 —

Now that we are becoming multisensory, a new psychology—spiritual psychology—is needed. The personality is specific aspects of the soul reduced to a physical form. Therefore, dysfunctions of the personality cannot be understood without an understanding of the soul. Psychology seeks to heal the personality without recognizing the force of the soul that lies behind the configuration and experiences of the personality and, therefore, cannot heal at the level of the soul. The characteristics of a personality cannot always be understood in terms of the history of the personality because they may reflect experiences that predate the personality, in some cases by centuries.

The healing power at the core of psychology is the power of consciousness. Seeking out, facing with courage, and bringing into the light of consciousness that which is unconscious and, therefore, in a position of power over the personality is what heals. When that which needs to be made conscious is not recognized to exist—such as experiences of lifetimes that were lived in other places and at other times—it cannot be healed in this way. Spiritual psychology will illuminate the relationship between the personality and the soul, make explicit the effects of interactions between personalities from the perspective of the impersonal energy dynamics that they set into motion, and show how these dynamics can be used to heal.

—— Psychology ——

Psychology means soul knowledge, but because five-sensory psychology does not recognize the existence of the soul, it cannot understand the soul's temperament, what it can and cannot tolerate, what contributes to its health, and what breaks its health down. The fears, angers, and jealousies that deform a personality cannot be understood apart from the karmic circumstances they serve. Without awareness of the experiences of other lifetimes of your soul, you cannot appreciate the potential awakenings that your interactions with others offer you. Your experiences are karmic necessities. When you realize this, you can choose not to react to them personally. When you engage in brutality, abundances of pain, irrationality, non-forgiveness, jealousies, hatreds, or lying to others, you diminish the strength of your soul, not to be confused with its immortality. Creating authentic power requires that you recognize the existence of your soul and grow in knowledge of what it is and what it wants.

Spiritual psychology is a disciplined and systematic study of these things.

If you are reading an eBook, click the following link to go to an expanded online version of this Chapter Study Guide, including video, meditation, and support for study groups. If you are reading a print copy, type it into your browser: www.seatofthesoul.com/sg13.

Questions

You can contribute to the creation of spiritual psychology, even if you do not have a degree in psychology. These questions will help you learn more about your soul and your relation to it. What other questions can you ask yourself?

1. *Have you seriously considered the existence of your soul?*

2. *Have you ever thought in terms of consciously assisting your soul in its evolution?*

3. *If you really believed that brutality, abundances of pain, irrationality, non-forgiveness, jealousies, hatreds, and lying to others prevent you from assisting your soul to evolve, would you think twice before indulging in them?*

4. *If your experiences really were karmic necessities, what could you accomplish by becoming upset with the people who bring them into your life?*

5. *How do you feel about the idea of living your life with an awareness of your soul and what would be best for it?*

Helpful Thought

Have you left a partner or a spouse? Has a spouse or a partner left you? It may be that your souls have graciously and with great compassion agreed to enact within this lifetime a situation that they have experienced together in another lifetime, or other lifetimes, a situation that still has healing potential for both. It may be that your souls have agreed to a mutual balancing of energy, so that one experiences the same painful loss that it inflicted previously upon the other. Experiences such as these are not meant to cause meaningless pain. There is not one act in the Universe that is not compassionate.

Exercise

Authentic Needs

When you strive to fulfill an artificial need, you are pursuing external power. A frightened part of your personality is controlling you. You strive to feel better about yourself and safe. If your need is artificial, you will be attached to having it met.

On the other hand, when you strive to fulfill your authentic needs, you are creating authentic power. You are choosing from a loving part of your personality that is in alignment with your soul and always strives to create authentic power. The Universe is that which fulfills your authentic needs, such as the need to grow spiritually, to cocreate for the common good, to love and be loved, and to contribute to Life.

It is easy to get caught in frightened parts of your personality and their artificial needs. Sometimes these parts of your personality are so familiar to you that they are very difficult to see unless you focus on becoming aware of them.

- *Set your intention each day to recognize the difference between your artificial needs and your authentic needs. The needs that come from frightened parts of your personality are artificial—they are means of manipulating and controlling. Your authentic needs are to love and be loved, to give the gifts that your soul wants to give, and to create authentic power, among others.*
- *Make a list of your authentic needs and your artificial needs this week. Let your intuition guide you in distinguishing between them.*
- *At the end of the week, write in your journal what you discovered regarding your authentic needs and your artificial needs. Give examples.*
- *What was the most surprising discovery you made about yourself and artificial needs versus authentic needs?*

— Chapter 14 —

Some traditions speak of life as an "illusion," but getting hit by a truck, becoming ill, and having your home foreclosed are very real events. How can we speak of concrete circumstances such as these as "illusions"? Each interaction with each individual and circumstance is part of a continual learning dynamic. This dynamic provides each individual at each moment a perfect opportunity to grow spiritually. Each interaction creates emotions within us, and each emotion is an experience of love or an experience of fear. Sooner or later—sometimes lifetimes later—we begin to see that acting on fear, such as anger, resentment, and jealousy, creates painful consequences (Law of Cause and Effect) and attracts others with these energies (Law of Attraction), and that when we act with love, such as gratitude, appreciation, patience, and caring, we create blissful consequences and also attract like energy. Eventually we become more interested in acting with love instead of with fear, regardless of what is happening around us, including accidents, illness, and foreclosures, and regardless of what is happening inside us, including anger, resentment, and jealousy. Eventually, we see *everything* as an opportunity to create with love instead of fear. This is spiritual growth. Fear creates the illusion that something should not have happened, that painful experiences are negative, and love dispels this illusion. Consciously using the illusion to grow spiritually is creating authentic power.

—— Illusion ——

The illusion allows each soul to perceive what it needs to understand in order to heal. The illusion for each soul is created by its intentions. A personality that lives in love and Light can see the illusion and not be drawn into it. Every experience of fear, anger, or jealousy is an illusion designed to bring your awareness to parts of your personality that require healing. The illusion has no power over you when you are fully aligned with your soul. Each personality attracts others with like consciousness. This is the Law of Attraction—anger attracts anger, greed attracts greed, compassion attracts compassion. Human emotions fall into two groups: love and fear. The illusion of each personality is generated by the frightened parts of its personality. The personality that follows a frightened part of itself chooses negative behavior, experiences the same behavior from another (this is the Law of Karma) and again receives the opportunity to release that negativity. This is how the illusion works.

If you are reading an eBook, click the following link to go to an expanded online version of this Chapter Study Guide, including video, meditation, and support for study groups. If you are reading a print copy, type it into your browser: www.seatofthesoul.com/sg14.

Questions

These questions can help you begin to look at the illusion from a different perspective. Take your time with them. Return to them frequently.

1. *When you are angry, how justified does your anger seem to you?*
2. *When you are jealous, how painful is your jealousy?*
3. *Have you ever considered that your painful emotions might be showing you parts of your personality that you need to heal?*
4. *What would your life be like if you were not controlled by the frightened parts of your personality?*
5. *What kind of people would you attract to you then?*

Exercises

The Illusions of Inferior and Superior

Recall someone you usually feel inferior to. It may be a friend, intimate partner, neighbor, family member, or anyone else. Recall a specific time when you felt inferior to this person. Notice the physical sensations in your energy centers, your thoughts, and your perceptions. See if you can recognize your intention toward this person.

Now recall someone you usually feel superior to. It may be a family member, friend, intimate partner, neighbor, or anyone else. Recall a specific time when you felt superior to this person. Notice the physical sensations in your energy centers, your thoughts, and your perceptions. See if you can recognize your intention toward this person.

Write in your journal what you discovered. If you are studying with someone, share what you learned with each other.

If I Were . . .

Before you speak or act, notice what you are feeling and where you are feeling it. For example, if you feel the need to please someone, focus your attention on your chest area, your throat area, and your solar plexus area. Notice whether or not you are feeling painful sensations in the vicinity of an energy-processing center. Give yourself a minute or more to do this.

Now think of a time you felt unconditionally loved. It may have been by a parent, friend, or relative. It may have been by the Universe. Give yourself a minute or more to do this. Focus your attention on your chest area, your throat area, and your solar plexus area. Notice whether or not you are experiencing good-feeling physical sensations in the vicinity of an energy-processing center.

Then ask yourself, "What would I say or do differently if I were worthy and adequate?"

(From *The Heart of the Soul* by Gary Zukav and Linda Francis)

Everything as an Opportunity

Practice seeing *everything* as an opportunity to create with love instead of fear, including all trauma and drama, for example, your favorite team losing a game, finding your car tire flat, your child getting into trouble at school, etc. Remember each time that your painful emotional reactions are part of an illusion that is offering you an opportunity to create with love instead of fear—to accelerate your spiritual growth.

— Chapter 15 —

At the heart of our unprecedented transformation from a five-sensory species that evolves by surviving into a multisensory species that evolves by growing spiritually is a new understanding of power. The old understanding is the ability to manipulate and control. The new understanding of power is the alignment of the personality with the soul. Multisensory perception and the new understanding of power cannot be separated. Multisensory perception is emerging within us whether or not we ask for it. Authentic power is our new potential. Each of us must create it for ourselves. Those who do not will continue unconsciously to manipulate and control and thereby unconsciously create violent and destructive consequences.

This is the new lay of the land. All of our old maps are obsolete. We are now evolving in uncharted territory. Our new polestar is the soul and its intentions—harmony, cooperation, sharing, and reverence for Life. Our tools are emotional awareness, responsible choice, and intuition. The new requirements of our evolution are commitment (to growing spiritually), courage (to enter our lives consciously), compassion (for ourselves and others), and conscious communications and actions that serve our spiritual development and support the spiritual development of others. Never before has a transformation of human *consciousness* occurred. Until now, the content of consciousness has changed. This is our history. Now our history, like a great river, has taken an abrupt plunge into new meaning, astonishing depth, immeasurable richness, and unimaginable fulfillment. Now is the time for us to swim in the great river consciously instead of being carried unconsciously through our lives by it, to see who is in the river with us, and to celebrate.

— Power —

Authentic power is energy that is formed by the intentions of the soul. It is Light shaped by love and compassion guided by wisdom. There is no power in fear or in any of the activities generated by fear. When energy leaves you in fear or distrust, you experience physical pain in your body near the energy centers that are losing power. For example, when you feel that you cannot care for or protect yourself, you feel pain or discomfort in your stomach area. When you feel you cannot give or receive love, you feel pain or discomfort in your chest area. Every physical dysfunction can be understood as a loss of power to an external circumstance or object through one of the seven energy centers in the body. When energy leaves you in any way except in strength and trust, it brings you only pain and discomfort. An authentically empowered human releases its energy only in love and trust. The characteristics of an authentically empowered personality are humbleness, forgiveness, clarity, and love.

If you are reading an eBook, click the following link to go to an expanded online version of this Chapter Study Guide, including video, meditation, and support for study groups. If you are reading a print copy, type it into your browser: www.seatofthesoul.com/sg15.

Questions

These questions will help you begin to look at power in a new way. Return to them as often as you think answering them will be helpful to you.

1. *Have you ever thought about power in terms of love, compassion, and wisdom?*
2. *Have you ever considered painful physical sensations such as heartache and anxiety as experiences of losing power?*
3. *Think of the people in your life that you consider to be the most powerful. Are they humble, forgiving, wise, and loving?*
4. *What does this tell you about the way you are thinking about power?*
5. *Are you powerful?*

Exercise

I Really Want to Learn This One

Pick a time when something happened that you had a strong reaction to. Perhaps you were very upset, angry, shocked, or deeply felt a loss. Did you cry, rage, feel confused, or withdraw and become very depressed? Remember how you acted. What physical sensations did you feel in your throat, chest, or solar plexus?

Close your eyes. Go back in your mind to that experience. This time, before you take action, feel the physical sensations in your body. Say to yourself, "I intend to learn the lessons my soul wants me to learn from this experience." Open yourself. Be patient. Give yourself time and don't expect that you will see immediately what you are to learn, although that is possible.

Open your eyes and write down what you discover.

(From *The Mind of the Soul* by Gary Zukav and Linda Francis)

Useful Diagram

Creating Authentic Power Transforms Your Life

FROM	TO
Experience	Experiment
Victim	Creator
Theories	Life of Meaning

(From *The Mind of the Soul* by Gary Zukav and Linda Francis)

Exercise

Using My Will

Recall a time when something happened and you had a strong reaction. For example, a time when you were very upset and you withdrew and cried, angry and you raged at the people you felt were at fault, shocked and you walked around confused for days, or deeply felt a loss and you became depressed for months. Remember how you acted and what you felt in your body, for example, the physical sensations you experienced in your throat, chest, and solar plexus.

Imagine that this time you get to make a new choice, that this time you can use your will to challenge the part of your personality that reacted habitually. As you recall this experience, experiment in your mind with making these choices:

- *Not to react while you are feeling the painful physical sensations in your body.*
- *To act with an intention of your soul while you are feeling the painful physical sensations in your body.*

Chapter 16

Trust is developed step by step. It requires openness to new thoughts, new ways of looking at things, and new ways of thinking. If openness is replaced by blind adherence to dogma, a fundamentalism is born instead of trust—rigid, demanding, righteous, and intimidating. Cliques, cultures, and congregations come into being that refuse to explore the endless diversity and boundless richness of Life and to experiment with love for self and others. Even cliques, cultures, and congregations that profess love become fortresses of fear. Trust in the compassion and wisdom of the Universe takes root in clarity, humbleness, forgiveness, and love—the characteristics of an authentically empowered personality. Multisensory perception is the species-wide game changer that is transforming trust in the wisdom and compassion of the Universe into the *perception* of the wisdom and compassion of the Universe. When even the most difficult circumstances, such as suffering, poverty, illness, cruelty, exploitation, and violence, become visible as opportunities to develop emotional awareness and responsible choice, to choose love instead of fear, to grow in joy and freedom, to create authentic power—where is the need for trust? All the gifts of the spirit appear in our lives—such as fellow humans with open hearts. A world of harmony, cooperation, sharing, and reverence for Life calls to us. We were born to bring that world into being.

— Trust —

Each soul enters into a sacred contract with the Universe before it incarnates. Authentic power is necessary to fulfill this contract. Only when you begin to fulfill your contract with the Universe will you become fulfilled. Each of your experiences helps waken you to your contract. They are not always experiences that you would choose. Your nonphysical Teachers continually support you. Delight in your dependency on them. Look at your life as a beautifully well-organized dynamic. Keep your power in the now. Challenge your fears. Set your intentions. Open to fellow humans. Pray. Prayer is moving into a personal relationship with Divine Intelligence. Say to the Universe, "Thy will be done," and take your hands off the steering wheel. Allow your life to go into the hands of the Universe completely. The final step in creating authentic power is releasing your own to a higher form of wisdom. Trust the Universe. Each of your choices serves the evolution of your soul perfectly. All roads lead to home. Trust allows bliss and laughter. Why not choose the road of bliss and laughter?

If you are reading an eBook, click the following link to go to an expanded online version of this Chapter Study Guide, including video, meditation, and support for study groups. If you are reading a print copy, type it into your browser: www.seatofthesoul.com/sg16.

Questions

1 What do you trust in your life?

2. If you are not sure that you trust the Universe, what would be your first step?

3. If you trust the Universe, what is the most significant example of your trust? If not, what is the most significant example of trust in the Universe you have heard about?

4. Do you know anything about your sacred contract? What do you feel you know about it? What do you feel it might be?

5. Are you aware of the support you are receiving from nonphysical Teachers? What is your most surprising example? If you are not aware of support you are receiving from nonphysical Teachers, are you willing to open to it?

Life Lesson

For the next week act as if you trusted the Universe to be wise and compassionate. Every time you encounter a difficult situation, person, or experience, remember to pay attention to the physical sensations you are feeling and the thoughts you are thinking. Then ask yourself:

- *If I trusted in the Universe, what would this help me to see about myself that is important for me to know or to learn? OR*
- *If I trusted the Universe, what strengths and clarity would this help me to develop? OR*
- *If I trusted the Universe, how would I see this differently?*

Ask the question that attracts you the most, or one that comes to you about how your life would change if you trusted the Universe. You can also ask yourself all these questions. Then listen for the answer or answers.

At the end of the week, write down the answers you have received.

Life Lesson

Imagine that what is in *The Seat of the Soul* is true, and that you intend to bring it alive in you in the deepest way possible. Spend the next several weeks rereading *The Seat of the Soul*, and, as you read, make notes about the parts of it that are now the most significant to you. Also write down questions that come up as you read, and open yourself to the deeper meaning of what you read. Go to parts of the book that you are drawn to or read it from beginning to end. Let your intuition guide you. Set your intention to see your next steps as you read, how you can change in the most constructive ways, and how the deepest meanings you see in *The Seat of the Soul* could come alive in you.

Spend some time each day reading. If possible, read out loud with someone. After you have reread *The Seat of the Soul*, use what you have learned to help you appreciate all that you have challenged and changed in yourself and what you have cultivated and strengthened in yourself since you began learning about authentic power.

Last, use this new perspective to support you in creating authentic power for the rest of your life.

Continue to be guided by this question as long as it is helpful to you:

> "How would I change my life if what is in
> *The Seat of the Soul*
> really were true?"

Index

addiction, 133–46
  acknowledgment of, 134, 295, 296,
    297, 298–99
  authentic power and, 294, 295, 299
  challenging of, 141–42, 294, 295
  choice and, 131, 140, 141–42,
    145–46, 294
  control by, 134
  definition of, 298
  Earth school and, 299
  exercise about, 296–97
  fear and, 294, 295, 297, 298, 299
  healing of, 139–46, 294, 295, 297
  as inadequacy, 139, 144
  intention and, 294, 298
  as irresponsible, 139
  Life Lesson about, 298–99
  as negativity, 136, 294
  personality and, 294, 295, 296, 298,
    299
  pleasure of, 144
  questions about, 296, 299
  rationalizations for, 133–34, 297–98
  second law of motion and, 139–40
  sexual, 135–38, 141, 144, 219, 221,
    295, 297
  spiritual evolution and, 145–46
  Study Guide for, 294–99
  temptation and, 139, 141
  Universal guidance about, 139, 143,
    144–45

afterlife, 149, 284, 307
AIDS, 137
alcoholism, 133, 138, 141, 144, 219,
  295
Angelic kingdom, 169
Angelou, Maya, 276
Angels, 167, 169–70, 171–72
anger, 23, 26, 32, 90
  authentic power and, 245
  compassion vs., 90
  effects of, 104–5, 153
  illusion and, 318, 319
  intention and, 281
  intuition and, 271
  Law of Attraction and, 318
  light frequency of, 200, 235, 274,
    275
  negative karma from, 201–2, 252,
    253
  power and, 325, 326
  psychology and, 313
  release of, 130
  sources of, 204
  trust and, 327
  understanding vs., 94
animal kingdom, 33, 37, 41, 162–63
anxiety, 211, 236, 324
archetypes, 109, 110, 112, 147–48, 149,
  151, 220, 300
army, 48
astrology, 193

INDEX

cycles of, 193
definition of, 3–4
fear and, 246, 306
of five-sensory personality, xxxi–
    xxxii, 4–10, 11–12, 17, 246, 263,
    288, 322
group influence on, 242
harmony as goal of, 150–51, 169, 189
horizontal vs. vertical path of,
    84–85, 129, 157, 219, 235–36
intention and, 288
and karma, 263
light and, 274
love and, 247, 306
of multisensory personality, xxxi–
    xxxii, 11–12, 16, 17–18, 247, 288,
    289, 322
organizational complexity in, 3–4
of physical form, 3–4
physical survival and, 246
pivot point in, 306
questions about, 247
reincarnation and, 30, 145–46
relationships and, 301
requirements for, 322–23
reverence and, 32–33, 36
self-, 289
self-sacrifice as evidence of, 4
of soul, 252, 263, 274, 284, 289, 290,
    295, 301, 306, 307, 329
speed of, 242
spiritual, 17–18, 84–85, 105, 109–10,
    145–46, 173–74, 181–82, 237–38
spiritual growth and, 322, 323
"survival of the fittest" in, 4, 6, 33
Study Guide about, 246
Universal, 193, 307
exercises:
    about addiction, 296–97
    about choice, 290–91
    about emotions, 265–66
    function/purpose of, 241
    about illusion, 319–20
    about intention, 280
    about intuition, 270
    about karma, 254–55
    about light, 276–77

about multisensory personalities, 248
about power, 324–25
about psychology, 314–16
about relationships, 302–3, 305
about reverence, 259–61
about soul, 309–10
external power, 246, 301, 315
    competition for, 9, 214–15
    definition of, 7–11
    domination and, 222
    fear and, 8–10, 11, 200–2, 209–10,
        211–13
    illusion and, 195–208
    perception of hierarchies from,
        8–10
    symbols of, 8–9, 214–15

failure, 204–5
fear:
    addiction and, 294, 295, 297, 298,
        299
    challenging, 233
    characteristics of, 262–63, 266
    choice and, 288, 293, 328
    clarity vs., 218–20
    collective, 160
    energy of, 275
    evolution and, 246, 306
    experience of, 80–81, 225–26
    identification of, 287
    illusion and, 317, 318, 319, 321
    intellect and, 266
    intention and, 281–82, 283, 284,
        286
    intuitions and, 73–74, 270, 271
    karma and, 285
    knowledge based on, 86–88, 106–7,
        123–24, 148–49, 150, 153, 194,
        236
    light and, 273, 274, 275
    and opening your heart, 266
    power and, 8–9, 10–11, 200–2, 209,
        210, 211–13, 245, 323
    as powerlessness, 199–202
    psychology and, 313, 315–16
    relationships and, 301, 302, 303,
        304, 305

About the Author

Gary Zukav is the author of four *New York Times* bestsellers, including the #1 *The Seat of the Soul* and *The Dancing Wu Li Masters*, winner of the American Book Award in Science. Six million copies of his books are in print and translations have been published in thirty-two languages. Gary Zukav grew up in the Midwest, graduated from Harvard, and became a Special Forces (Green Beret) officer with Vietnam service before writing his first book. He lives in Oregon with his spiritual partner, Linda Francis. For more information about Gary Zukav visit www.seatofthesoul.com.